# The System Design Interview

*Featuring the PEDALS Method*™

# LEWIS C. LIN
# SHIVAM P. PATEL

## ALSO BY LEWIS C. LIN

*71 Brilliant Salary Negotiation Email Samples*

*Case Interview Questions for Tech Companies*

*Decode and Conquer*

*How to Be a Great Product Manager*

*Interview Math*

*The Marketing Interview*

*The Product Manager Interview*

*Secrets of the Product Manager Interview*

Copyright © 2022 by Lewis C. Lin. All rights reserved. No part of this publication may be reproduced, distributed, or transmitted in any form or by any electronic or mechanical means including information storage and retrieval systems without the prior written permission from the publisher.

Published by Impact Interview, 115 North 85th St., Suite 202, Seattle, WA 98103.

Several fictitious examples have been used in this book; these examples involve names of real people, places and organizations. Any slights of people, places, or organizations are unintentional.

The author and publisher have made every effort to ensure the accuracy and completeness of information contained in this book. However, we assume no responsibility for errors, inaccuracies, omissions, or any inconsistency herein.

Corporations, organizations and educational institutions: bulk quantity pricing is available. For information, contact lewis@impactinterview.com.

SECOND EDITION / Tenth Printing

Lin, Lewis C. and Shivam P. Patel
The System Design Interview / Lewis C. Lin and Shivam P. Patel.

# Table of Contents

**INTRODUCTION** ................................................................ 10

**CHAPTER 1 THE SYSTEM DESIGN INTERVIEW** ................... 14

Why Are System Design Questions Asked? ........................................................ 15

What Interviewers Look For in a Response ........................................................ 17

Who Gets System Design Questions? .................................................................. 18

**CHAPTER 2 THE PEDALS™ FRAMEWORK** ............................ 21

What is PEDALS™? .................................................................................................. 21

**CHAPTER 3 PROCESS REQUIREMENTS** ................................ 22

The Importance of Understanding the Interviewer's Expectations ............ 22

Vague Requests Reflect Real-World Reality ...................................................... 23

Practice Questions ................................................................................................... 24

**CHAPTER 4 ESTIMATE** ............................................................. 25

Why Do Interviewers Ask Estimation Questions? ........................................... 26

How to Approach ..................................................................................................... 26
    Estimating Servers Needed ............................................................................. 26
    Estimating Storage Needed ............................................................................ 27
    Estimating Bandwidth Needed ...................................................................... 28

Assumptions to Know and Memorize ................................................................ 29

Practice Questions ................................................................................................... 31

**CHAPTER 5 DESIGN THE SERVICE: BASIC STRATEGIES** ..... 32

Defining the What ........................................................................................... 32
    Introducing CRUD ..................................................................................... 32
    Tip: Demystifying Update in CRUD ....................................................... 33

Describing the How ........................................................................................ 34

Mistakes to Avoid When Designing Services ............................................ 35
    Mistake #1: Not involving the interviewer ............................................. 35
    Mistake #2: Diving into the minutiae ...................................................... 36
    Mistake #3: Talking too long ..................................................................... 37

Be RESTful: API Best Practices .................................................................... 38
    API Tip #1: Use Nouns ............................................................................... 39
    API Tip #2: Use nesting to show the hierarchy ..................................... 40
    API Tip #3: Use plural ................................................................................ 40
    API Tip #4: Support filtering and pagination ........................................ 40
    API Tip #5: Return JSON ........................................................................... 40

## CHAPTER 6 DESIGN THE SERVICE: ADVANCED STRATEGIES .................................................................................................. 42

Introducing Design Strategies ...................................................................... 42

Design Strategies You Need to Know ......................................................... 42
    Information Processing Strategies ........................................................... 42
    Rate Limiting Strategies ............................................................................. 44
    Communication Strategies ........................................................................ 47
    Latency Strategies ....................................................................................... 49
    Efficiency Strategies ................................................................................... 53
    Space Reduction Strategies ....................................................................... 54
    Synchronization Strategies ....................................................................... 55
    Error Handling Strategies ......................................................................... 56
    Code Readability, Maintainability, and Elegance Strategies ............... 57
    Security Strategies ...................................................................................... 59

Practice Questions ......................................................................................... 61

## CHAPTER 7 ARTICULATE THE DATA MODEL ...................... 62

Tables ................................................................................................................ 62

Fields ................................................................................................................. 63

Database Storage ............................................................................................ 63
    SQL Databases ........................................................................................ 64
    NoSQL Databases ................................................................................... 65
    The Main Difference Between SQL and NoSQL ...................................... 65
    How to Choose Between SQL and NoSQL ............................................... 66
    Frequently Asked Questions: NoSQL vs. SQL ........................................... 66

Non-Database Storage .................................................................................... 67

Practice Questions ........................................................................................... 68

## CHAPTER 8 LIST THE ARCHITECTURAL COMPONENTS ..... 69

Introduction to Architecture ........................................................................... 69

Service-Oriented Architecture ......................................................................... 71

Architecture Verification ................................................................................. 71

Basics of System Architecture Diagrams ........................................................ 72
    Standard Visuals ..................................................................................... 72
    Architectural Generalizations ................................................................. 73
    Component Relationships ....................................................................... 75

## CHAPTER 9 SCALE ............................................................. 76

How to Tackle Common Scale Issues ............................................................. 76
    Problem: Handling More Users and User Requests ............................... 77
    Problem: Handling More Data Reads .................................................... 78

Additional Solutions for Solving Scale Issues ................................................ 81
    Problem: Avoiding Crashes .................................................................... 81
    Problem: Providing Data Consistency ................................................... 81
    Problem: Need to Improve Latency ........................................................ 82

Identifying and Alleviating Scalability Bottlenecks ........................................ 83
    Less than 1,000 Users ............................................................................. 84
    1K to 10K Users ...................................................................................... 85
    100K Users .............................................................................................. 86
    500K Users .............................................................................................. 87
    One Million Users .................................................................................. 87

Practice Questions ........................................................................................... 89

## CHAPTER 10 EXAMPLE CASES ................................................. 90

Design Twitter ........................................................................... 90

Design Instagram ..................................................................... 103

Design TinyURL ...................................................................... 115

Design YouTube ....................................................................... 127

Design WhatsApp .................................................................... 139

Design Unique ID Generator ................................................. 151

Design Auto-Suggest................................................................ 161

Design an Air Traffic Controller ........................................... 176

## CHAPTER 11 CONCEPTS YOU SHOULD KNOW ................ 186

Service Design and APIs ........................................................ 186
    Application Programming Interface (API) ..................... 186
    Atomic Operations ............................................................ 187
    Backpressure ...................................................................... 187
    Callback Functions ........................................................... 187
    Concurrency....................................................................... 188
    Containers.......................................................................... 189
    Daemon Services............................................................... 189
    Fan Out ............................................................................... 190
    Event-Driven Programming............................................. 190
    Hashing ............................................................................... 190
    JSON................................................................................... 191
    Locality............................................................................... 191
    Logical Design................................................................... 191
    Machine Learning ............................................................. 192
    Message Queues ................................................................ 194
    Microservice Architecture ............................................... 196
    Natural Language Processing.......................................... 197
    Pipeline .............................................................................. 197
    Polling ................................................................................ 197
    Postman ............................................................................. 197
    Proxies ................................................................................ 198
    Publish and Subscribe ..................................................... 201

- Remote Procedure Calls .......... 201
- Serialization .......... 201
- Software Development Kit (SDK) .......... 201
- Stack vs. Heap .......... 202
- Stacks vs. Queues .......... 202
- Tech Debt .......... 203
- XML .......... 203

## Databases, data storage, and data models .......... 203
- ACID .......... 203
- Apache Cassandra .......... 204
- CAP Theorem .......... 204
- Database Index .......... 205
- Eventual Consistency .......... 206
- Flat File .......... 206
- Object Storage .......... 207
- NoSQL .......... 207
- SQL .......... 207

## Cloud Architecture .......... 209
- Application Server .......... 209
- Cloud Terms .......... 209
- HTTP .......... 212
- Internet Protocol (IP) .......... 212
- IP Address .......... 212
- IP Packet .......... 213
- Physical Design .......... 214
- Transmission Control Protocol (TCP) .......... 214
- User Datagram Protocol (UDP) .......... 216
- Web Servers .......... 216

## Scaling .......... 216
- Caching .......... 216
- Chaos Engineering .......... 218
- Content Delivery Network (CDN) .......... 219
- Data Centers .......... 220
- Distributed Cache .......... 220
- Federation .......... 220
- Hadoop Distributed File System (HDFS) .......... 221
- Horizontal and Vertical Scaling .......... 222
- MapReduce .......... 223
- Sharding .......... 224
- Zookeeper (Apache) .......... 224

## CHAPTER 12 FREQUENTLY ASKED QUESTIONS .......... 225

# CHAPTER 13 SOLUTIONS ................................................... 231

Answers: Process Requirements Section ..................................................... 231

Answers: Estimate Section ............................................................................. 231

Answers: Design the Service Section ........................................................... 238

Answers: Articulate the Data Model Section .............................................. 243

Answers: Scale Section .................................................................................. 247

# WHAT'S NEXT ................................................................. 248

# ACKNOWLEDGMENTS ................................................... 249

# Introduction

The system design interview tests your ability to design scalable software systems. We'll call it "system design" for short. Some popular interview examples include *Build Instagram* or *Build Google Maps*.

If you're reading the book, we're assuming you took an intro computer science (CS) course at some point in your career. Your instructor may have given you the assignment to build a social media app like Instagram. Given that experience, you may wonder, "How is answering the *Build Instagram* interview question any different?"

The biggest difference: guidance. Your instructor's help made it easy. She provided a starting point like the initial code, libraries, and graphic assets. She gave you a detailed, battle-tested assignment sheet with little ambiguity. All of this made it easier to finish. It's the CS equivalent of painting-by-numbers.

## System Design Tests Your Ability to Program in the Real World

Professional artists don't paint-by-numbers and neither do software engineers or technical professionals. Here's why:

- **Customized nature of software**. One-of-a-kind customer and business requirements mean custom code. Reusable code and services can only do so much.
- **Speed of innovation**. We can't rest on our successes for long. We're constantly moving toward building the next big thing. These new systems rarely have overlap with systems we've built in the past.
- **Limited team bandwidth**. Bosses and peers are busy solving their own technical challenges. As a result, they don't have time to assist others. Ever wonder why bosses love "self-starters" that can cope in "ambiguous environments?" To them, the best problem solvers are those who solve problems on their own.

## Why System Design Seems Impossible

You might be wondering, "How can interviewers expect us to build popular apps in a 45-minute interview when it took years to do so?"

We're with you. System design is intimidating. Our friends' advice does little to reassure us. Their advice ranges from the generic to the cynical:

| Advice Type | What It Sounds Like |
|---|---|
| Generic | "Start broad then go deep, peeling back layers of the onion as you go along." OR "Start with the end in mind and work your way toward the result." |
| Jargon-Filled | "Just think SDLC (software development lifecycle). Start with the idea then feasibility, analysis, requirements analysis, systems analysis, specs, system design, development testing, implementation, maintenance, and finally review." |
| Cynical | "There's no way you can prepare for this. Experience is the only way to learn system design." |

## How to Get the Most Out of this Book

The first chapter introduces the system design interview. Next, we introduce the most valuable part of the book: the PEDALS Method™. PEDALS is a six-step method to help you make your way through any SDI question.

Think of PEDALS as that recipe or map that guides you through a system design question from start to finish. By using PEDALS, the odds that your answer is complete, satisfying, and memorable increase substantially.

To build your system design muscle, we've created a series of mini exercises for each PEDALS step.

Finally, toward the end of the book, you'll appreciate our complete answers for the most popular system design questions. You may have heard people say that a good SDI response feels like a conversation. That's what makes our book unique: it includes turn-by-turn conversational dynamics.

It takes talent to manage the system design conversation. Stronger candidates can:

- Get critical information without appearing dumb or naïve.
- Respond to criticism without sounding defensive.
- Share solutions and insights without coming across as arrogant.

As you read our answers, you'll discover how to manage difficult interviewers.

We encourage you to follow, understand, and analyze the conversational dialogue. Over time, you'll use and adapt the same conversational tactics and impress your interviewers. You'll convince them that you're not only capable but also a good fit.

## Conventions in the Book

The book deals with large numbers in the thousands, millions, and billions. To save space, we will use the following abbreviations:

- K = thousands
- M = millions
- B = billions

For instance, 10K refers to 10,000. 10M is equal to 10,000,000, and 10B is equal to 10,000,000,000.

Next, we'll use units of measure for space and time. Here are some that you should memorize:

### Units of Storage

| Abbreviation | Full Name | Approximate Value in Bytes* |
|---|---|---|
| KB | Kilobyte | One thousand |
| MB | Megabyte | One million |
| GB | Gigabyte | One billion |
| TB | Terabyte | One trillion |
| PB | Petabyte | One quadrillion |
| EB | Exabyte | One quintillion |

* A byte consists of 8 bits.

### Units of Time

1 ns (nanosecond) = $10^{-9}$ seconds

1 $\mu s$ (microsecond) = $10^{-6}$ seconds = 1,000 ns

1 ms (millisecond) = $10^{-3}$ seconds = 1,000 us = 1,000,000 ns

**Inclusive Terms**

We'll use inclusive terms, recommended by W3C, instead of traditional terms:

| Inclusive Term We Use | Traditional Term We Avoid |
|---|---|
| main or primary | master |
| replica or secondary | slave |
| allowlist | whitelist |
| denylist | blacklist |

Lastly, for the sake of simplicity, we refer to hypothetical candidates as "he." We will refer to other characters, such as hypothetical interviewers, as "she."

## Two More Things

Learning and practicing on your own, along with reading this book, is a great start. However, nobody has won a karate tournament by reading a book. You must practice with others.

Join Lewis' Slack group to find mock interview partners. Those partners will provide something that this book cannot: feedback on how well you're applying the concepts you've learned from this book. You'll also benefit from their unique perspectives. To sign up, search for "Lewis Lin Slack" on Google.

We're always interested in hearing from readers. To send a note, ask a question, or report typos email lewis@impactinterview.com.

# Chapter 1 The System Design Interview

Every software engineering interview has two components: the technical and non-technical interview.

The non-technical part consists of behavioral questions and icebreakers like *Tell me about yourself*. But let's focus our attention on the technical part. In the past, the technical interview would consist of only coding interview questions. Coding interviews test your ability to write clean code, conjure clever algorithms, and choose efficient data structures.

Today's technical interviews are different. Half the time you'll get a traditional coding interview question. The other half of the time you'll get a mysterious system design question. Here are some recent instances:

- *Design Twitter.*
- *Design a URL shortener.*
- *Design an auto-suggest or type-ahead service.*

System design questions focus on building an application or system. It starts with the big picture. The conversation then branches into more detailed areas including:

- Describing the API endpoints
- Specifying the database schema
- Estimating total storage needed
- Recommending the type of storage
- Suggesting how to scale a system

System design questions aren't algorithm questions. An algorithm question sounds like *Find the longest substring without repeating characters.*

Here's how system design and algorithm questions differ:

|  | System Design | Coding |
|---|---|---|
| Scope | Cover the entire system. | Cover a small subcomponent. |
| Whiteboard Coding | Rarely. | Required. |
| Question Clarity | Open-ended and vague. The candidate is responsible for clarifying, scoping, and otherwise "owning" the question's direction. | Better defined and less open-ended when compared to system design questions. |
| No Clear "Right" Answer | No unquestioned "right" answer. Conversations can evolve differently and lead to different acceptable answers.<br><br>System design questions are also subjective. Some interviewers have preferences for particular design choices and solutions. | Usually have a commonly accepted "right" answer. |
| Conversational Dynamics Matter | Your reaction to your interviewer's follow-up questions and criticism matters. Do you wilt or go silent? Or do you assertively address them? | More like math problems; you solve and then explain your solution. |

# Why Are System Design Questions Asked?

If you answered, "It's part of the job," then you're correct. Software engineers *code*, but they also *design* software that:

- Is inexpensive to build
- Is easy to maintain
- Handles the expected number of users
- Responds quickly
- Scales easily

The interviewer wants to be confident that you can build systems on the job. Speaking of what you need to do on the job, let's look at a software engineering job description:

*Title*
*Software Engineer, Google*

*About the job*
*Google's software engineers develop next-generation technologies that*

change how **billions of users** connect, explore, and interact with information and one another. Our products need to **handle information at a massive scale** and extend well beyond web search. We're looking for engineers who bring fresh ideas from all areas, including information retrieval, **distributed computing**, **large-scale system design**, networking and data storage, security, artificial intelligence, natural language processing, UI design and mobile; the list goes on and is growing every day. As a software engineer, you will work on a specific project critical to Google's needs with opportunities to switch teams and projects as you and our fast-paced business grow and evolve. We need our engineers to be versatile, display leadership qualities and be enthusiastic to take on new problems across the entire stack as we continue to push technology forward.

Google is and always will be an engineering company. We hire people with a broad set of technical skills who are ready to take on some of technology's greatest challenges and **make an impact on millions, if not billions, of users**. At Google, engineers not only revolutionize search, they routinely work on **massive scalability** and storage solutions, **large-scale applications** and entirely new platforms for developers around the world. From Google Ads to Chrome, Android to YouTube, Social to Local, Google engineers are changing the world one technological achievement after another.

## Scale Is Key With Modern App Development

We see that Google is looking for smart folks with a strong grasp of computer science. But focus on the phrases we've bolded. You'll notice a critical theme: a demonstrated ability to build applications *at scale*.

The software engineer's role has evolved since the desktop era. Back then, most developers created applications for a single PC, serving a single user. If the application was too slow, the developer could chide the user to buy a more powerful machine.

Today's developers create apps that connect to the Internet, serving billions of people. To serve billions, apps work across hundreds and perhaps thousands of computers.

As a result, making an Internet app more responsive isn't as easy as asking a user to upgrade their PC. Instead, it could involve:

- Adding *load balancers*
- Implementing *server-side caches*
- Upgrading *distributed database systems*

### System Design Is Hard

Here's why system design questions are so challenging:

- **Time pressure.** In the real world, a well-thought-out system is rarely built in a day, let alone a 45-minute system design interview.
- **Domain expertise.** Experience counts. Answering an SDI question about messaging systems is easier for someone who's done it before. Most new graduates do not have this advantage.
- **Individual, not a team, effort.** Anyone who's built a complicated system knows that it's not a one-person endeavor. Instead, you benefit from the opinions of your manager, colleagues, or technical architects. During the SDI, your only source of advice is the typically tight-lipped interviewer.
- **Unpredictability.** The system design conversation can unfold in unpredictable ways. It may be unclear what the interviewer wants you to address; the interviewer may also have hidden goals and personal pet peeves that can derail the conversation.

## What Interviewers Look For in a Response

Here's how hiring managers distinguish between those who excel and those who do not:

| Performance Level | Indicators |
|---|---|
| Unsatisfactory | <ul><li>Does not ask questions.</li><li>Constantly veers into irrelevant design issues.</li><li>Assumes it's someone else's job to design a system.</li></ul> |

| | |
|---|---|
| Marginal | - Fails to ask the right questions.
- Does not collaborate with the interviewer.
- Given hint(s), the candidate can complete the design task.
- Doesn't spend enough time planning, leading to an inefficient design.
- Candidate makes a marginal contribution to clarifying the requirements. |
| Competent | - Thinks through failure cases.
- Proactively leads the scoping and implementation of the system.
- Completes the question with minimal guidance.
- Breaks down a large feature, product, or feature into sub-tasks.
- Identifies risks and constraints first.
- Given an introduction completes the design of small and medium-sized features. |
| Excellent | - Anticipates technical challenges, exploring alternatives and tradeoffs thoroughly.
- Designs for scale and reliability with the future in mind.
- Successfully scopes, designs, and delivers solutions for large, complex systems.
- Systematically thinks through potential design impacts on other teams and the company.
- Makes well-reasoned design decisions, identifying potential issues, tradeoffs, risks, and the appropriate level of abstraction.
- Understands implications and trade-offs of reliability, scalability, operational costs, and ease of adoption.
- Given an (intentionally) large and poorly understood problem, can explore the solution space to determine the correct course of action.
- Given a medium to large understood problem, can design and implement a solution. |
| Exceptional | - Can lay out a path across many versions, given long term strategic goals. |

## Who Gets System Design Questions?

*Software architects* should expect system design questions. That's their job.

*Software engineers* should expect them too. Technical roles have flattened over the years: many companies have phased out architect, test, and dev ops roles. Most companies expect *experienced* engineers to take on a broad array of responsibilities including system design.

Lastly, we see some companies give system design questions to *entry-level engineers*. This happens less often than interviews with experienced candidates.

However, we expect that to change. Hiring managers anticipate entry-level candidates will soon get system design questions at the same frequency as experienced engineers. Why? We're all building Internet applications that must be ready to scale.

## Who else gets these questions?

Those who aren't software engineers may have heard they should anticipate system design questions including:

- Product Managers
- Technical Program Managers
- QA Tester
- Data Scientists
- Data Engineers
- Support Engineers

If you fit in one of these categories, you may be thinking: *Why would I need to know system design if that's not my job?*

Building a meaningful application is not an individual endeavor. The ones who code *rely on others* for the following:

- What are the inputs and outputs?
- What are the edge and corner cases?
- What are the potential solution alternatives?
- And the ultimate question: is the system built correctly?

In other words, system design questions can also test whether non-coders can collaborate effectively with the coders.

| The Interviewer Is Evaluating Whether You... | ...So That the Developer Can |
|---|---|
| Can specify system requirements? | Get clear feature input |
| Can articulate and verify system behavior? | Understand the feature's output |
| Can specify constraints? | Cover edge and corner cases |
| Can contribute to technical brainstorming? | Approach the system design with the optimal solution |
| Can you point out technical drawbacks? | Build bug-free systems |

For the non-coders, discussing technical details can create anxiety and fear. Ultimately, we agree with the hiring managers: the more adept you are at discussing how technical systems are built, the more effective you'll be in partnering with them.

# Chapter 2 The PEDALS™ Framework

## What is PEDALS™?

PEDALS™ is a six-step framework to help you answer any system design question. It's a checklist to help your response come across as complete and thoughtful. It's also a memory aid that saves us from missing a critical discussion point. PEDALS™ stands for:

**P** rocess Requirements

**E** stimate

**D** esign the Service

**A** rticulate the Data Model

**L** ist the Architectural Components

**S** cale

We'll discuss each one of the six steps in detail, starting with process requirements. And in case you forget, remember that cyclists pedal their way through a race, and PEDALS™ can power you through your system design interview.

# Chapter 3 Process Requirements

The first step of PEDALS is process requirements. When we say this, what we mean is *clarify the question*.

Clarifying starts by understanding the product you're trying to build:

- What is it?
- What features does it include?
- How does it work?

Another way to think about it: What *job* is the system doing?

We call this a user story. The user story format is as follows:

*As a <user>, I want <feature> so that I can get <benefit>.*

When gathering requirements, it's natural to ask questions. Do not panic if the interviewer doesn't answer. Instead, assume based on what you know. Then allow the interviewer an opportunity to correct you if she thinks differently.

Here are the key questions you must ask:

- What are the goals or outcomes?
- What are the constraints?
- What features should be included? And what features should be left out?

If it's appropriate, you may also want to ask whether your interviewer expects you to:

- Write code on the whiteboard?
- Draw system flow diagrams?
- Or give a verbal solution?

## The Importance of Understanding the Interviewer's Expectations

A question can be as short as *Design Twitter*.

Here's the interesting thing: all candidates, including experienced ones, tend to answer *without clarifying.* That's not good.

## Clarification avoids disappointment

Why the need for clarification?

Let's consider the question *Design Twitter*. Does the interview mean that literally? Or perhaps a social media platform that's inspired by it?

Next, how much time do you have? An hour? 30 minutes? Or less?

Additionally, is it just a news feed feature? How about direct messages? Sign-up? Authentication? How about photo and even video storage?

Here's what happens to candidates who don't clarify: they fail to answer interviews' hidden questions and expectations. The answer will be too long or too curt. They'll miss a subsystem the interviewer wanted to discuss.

Misfiring on the interviews' expectations will disappoint or frustrate them. Unhappy hiring managers do not give job offers.

# Vague Requests Reflect Real-World Reality

These short, vague questions reflect what happens on the job. During a meeting, an executive may blurt out: "I want you to compete with Twitter!"

Imagine telling her that you ignored her command because you felt it was incomplete or unclear. Do you think she's going to be pleased?

Incomplete, unclear requests abound in the real world. SD questions give candidates a chance to prove that they CAN *make sense* of and *take action* in an ambiguous world.

Lastly, there are a few reasons why we forget to clarify:

### Adrenaline

When we get a command or request, we're eager to do *something*. Pause too long, and the interview may think we don't know or slow-witted. Reacting quickly seems like a blessing when it is often a curse!

### Lack of Knowledge

Less experienced folks haven't built the system before, so they often don't know what questions to ask.

### Lack of Practice

Some people, especially those whose experience has been limited to the academic environment, may not have practice clarifying questions.

Why? Vague school assignments are not normal. If there's any ambiguity, it's more work for the professor. She'll take on unnecessary work to clarify what she means.

## Practice Questions

What clarifying questions would you ask for these design prompts?

1. Design a ride-sharing system.
2. Design a professional social network.
3. Create a competitor to AWS, GCP, or Azure.

*See the Solutions chapter for answers.*

# Chapter 4 Estimate

The second step of PEDALS is to estimate.

It's always a good idea to estimate the scale of your system as this will later provide more clarity when you begin designing your system. Estimations will also offer interviewers insight as to whether your architected system will fulfill the functional requirements. These requirements might include:

- Number of total users
- Number of active users
- Requests per second (RPS)
- Logins per seconds
- Storage needed

You may also need to understand:

- E-commerce: Transactions per second
- Social media sites: Likes per second, shares per second, comments per second
- Sites with a search feature: Searches per second

In our experience, approximately 20 percent of interviews will ask you to perform some sort of estimation. Other times, interviewers will simply provide the details to save time. They might say something along the lines of: *Your system should...*

- *Support 100M concurrent users*
- *Store 10 exabytes of photos*
- *Process 1M e-commerce transactions per hour*

If you're given an estimation question, your interviewer might ask you to estimate anything from user demand, such as the number of expected users, to the expected number of operations, such as Tweets per hour.

You could also be asked to estimate *system requirements*, such as the number of servers or storage needed such as servers or storage needed to support Google Maps.

You can think of this "E"stimate step as part of clarifying requirements. The user demand, servers needed, and other system requirements will be particularly helpful during the sixth step of PEDALS: scaling.

As you can imagine, your scaling recommendations will likely be very different if you were to support one user vs. one million. So, it's crucial to clarify these requirements.

## Why Do Interviewers Ask Estimation Questions?

When the interview does ask you to estimate, what are they trying to evaluate? They want to see your ability to approximate a value.

We can't blame if you want to say, "I don't know" or "You work at Google, why don't you tell me?" Doing so would miss the interviewer's point. She's trying to understand your:

- **Analytical abilities**. Do you feel comfortable calculating numbers?
- **Judgment**. Do you make reasonable assumptions?
- **Communication skills**. Are your explanations easy to follow? Can you persuade the interviewer that your assumptions are valid?

## How to Approach

When it comes to estimations, here are three frameworks to help you prepare:

- Estimating Servers Needed
- Estimating Storage Needed
- Estimating Bandwidth Needed

### Estimating Servers Needed

When asked to estimate servers needed, approach in the following manner:

1. Work per single CPU core. How much work can a single CPU core handle?
2. Work per server. Multiply that single-core number by the # of CPU cores per server.
3. The number of servers. Multiply that number by the number of servers.

We'll do a quick example:

### Step 1. Work per Single CPU Core.
Let's say you determine that a particular task takes 10 ms to complete.

10 milliseconds is 0.01 seconds. So that means a single-core CPU can handle 100 requests per second.

### Step 2. Work per Server.
Let's assume the server has 32 cores. Hence, the server can handle 3,200 requests per second (32 cores * 100 requests per second per core).

### Step 3. Number of Servers.
Let's say we need to handle 100,000 requests per second (RPS). To find the number of servers we need, we just divide the goal, 100,000 RPS, by how much the server can handle per second, which is 3,200 requests.

This means we need 31.25 servers.

## Estimating Storage Needed

When asked to estimate storage needed, approach as follows:

1. Determine the different data types.
2. Estimate space needed for each type.
3. Add and multiply to get the total space needed.

To illustrate the approach, we'll estimate the amount of storage YouTube stores daily. We'll focus on estimating the storage required and not worry about the data consumed.

### Step 1. Determine the data types.
- Videos

- Thumbnail images
- Comments

## Step 2. Estimate the space needed for each.
Let's assume that YouTube has roughly 1B users. 5 percent upload videos consistently, leaving us with 50M YouTube uploaders.

### Videos
Let's guestimate that, on average, a YouTube creator uploads 10 videos annually. That's 500M videos uploaded annually and roughly 1.3M videos daily. A video about 10 minutes long at 1080p would roughly be about 4GB.

We should assume that YouTube will compress videos. Let's say a compressed 4GB video takes only 40MB of space.

### Thumbnails
Let's also say that each video has a thumbnail image consisting of 20KB.

### Comments
Finally, let's say each video has an average of five comments.

Let's say each comment is 100 bytes long: 100 bytes per comment * 5 comments = 500 bytes per video.

## Step 3. Find total storage needed.
Summing up the estimated storage for each component, we find that each uploaded video requires approximately ~40MB of space (40MB + 20KB + 500 bytes). Multiplying this with 1.3M videos uploaded daily (40MB * 1.3 M), we find that YouTube will require approximately 52TB of storage on a given day.

# Estimating Bandwidth Needed
If asked to take our estimation a step further:

When estimating bandwidth:

1. Determine incoming data to the server in a day.
2. Determine total outgoing data from the server in a day.

3. Divide both incoming and outgoing data to estimate bandwidth.

Carrying on from our YouTube example, we would estimate bandwidth as follows:

### Step 1. Determine incoming data.
As we already estimated earlier, YouTube requires roughly 52TB of storage in a given day.

### Step 2. Determine total outgoing data.
Now, let's say that 10% of YouTube's user base are daily active users. With approximately 100M daily users, let's also assume that a daily user watches about 10 videos in a day. Based on this assumption, we would estimate that YouTube would receive roughly 1B views in a day (100M daily users * 10 views). If every view required the viewer to download a 40MB video, this would result in a total of 40PB of outgoing data in a given day.

### Step 3. Divide both incoming and outgoing data to estimate bandwidth
We can determine the incoming data by dividing this number by the number of seconds in a day (52TB / 86,400 seconds). Converting this into GB, we find that YouTube experiences upload speeds at about 0.6 GB per second.

If we divide our total outgoing data by the number of seconds in a day (40PB / 86,400), we find that YouTube experiences processing speeds at roughly 460GB per second.

## Assumptions to Know and Memorize
When estimating, assumptions can be a challenge.

Here are some common assumptions that you should memorize. Also, when anticipating questions for your upcoming system design interview, take the research, in advance, any assumptions you might need, including ones not listed here.

## Storage Assumptions

### Images

| Quality | Size | Example |
|---|---|---|
| Low | 20 KB | Thumbnails |
| Medium | 200 KB | Most website images |
| High | 2 MB | Most smartphone images |

### Video

| Quality | Size | Example |
|---|---|---|
| Low | 256 MB | One-minute 720p video |
| Medium | 403MB | One-minute 1080p video |
| High | 2GB | One-minute 4K video |

### Other Media

| Type | Size |
|---|---|
| eBook | 1 to 5 MB |
| MP3 quality song | 3 to 4 MB |

## Latency Assumptions

### Network Latency

| Operation | Time | Description |
|---|---|---|
| 1 InterPacket | 150 ms | Send 1 packet from US to Europe |
| One IntraPacket | 70 ms | Send 1 packet from SF to NYC |
| 1MB Network | 10 ms | Read 1 MB from 1 Gbps network |

### Disk Latency

| Operation | Time | Description |
|---|---|---|
| Disk | 2 ms | Seek from disk |
| 1MB Disk | 0.625 ms | Read 1 MB from disk |
| SSD | 0.016 ms | Seek from SSD |
| 1MB SSD | 0.03 ms | Read 1MB from SSD |

### Memory Latency

| Operation | Time | Description |
|---|---|---|
| Memory | 100 ns | Seek from memory |
| 1MB Memory | 2,000 ns | Read 1MB from memory |

### Cache Latency

| Operation | Time | Description |
|---|---|---|
| L2 cache | 4 ns | Seek from L2 cache |
| L1 cache | 1 ns | Seek from L1 cache |

Do note that a nanosecond is 1,000,000 times faster than a millisecond! Avoid fetching from disk or network, if you can.

## Practice Questions

1. How many transactions does Amazon have per second in the USA?
2. How many Google searches are executed per second?
3. How many WhatsApp messages are transmitted per second in the USA?
4. How much space does Instagram need for its photos on a given day?
5. How much storage space does Twitter need on a given day?

*See the Solutions chapter for answers.*

# Chapter 5 Design the Service: Basic Strategies

The third step of PEDALS is to outline the system's functionality. We call that designing the service, and there are two parts.

1. Figure out what to build
2. How to build it

## Defining the What

Step 1 of PEDALS, clarifying the requirements, should have given you a sense of what features and capabilities you need for the service.

If you're still struggling to define components of the service, we've got a framework to help fill the missing details: CRUD.

### Introducing CRUD

CRUD stands for:

| C | reate |
|---|---|
| R | ead |
| U | pdate |
| D | elete |

Each letter in CRUD corresponds with a possible system action. Let's say we're building a YouTube-like video service. We can use CRUD to help brainstorm possible system actions:

| Type | Possible User Actions |
|---|---|
| Create | Upload **videos**<br>Add **comments**<br>Create new **users**<br>Create a **channel** |
| Read | View **videos**<br>Read **comments**<br>See video **recommendations**<br>**Search** for videos |
| Update | Edit **comments**<br>Edit **video** metadata |
| Delete | Delete **videos**<br>Delete **comments** |

| | |
|---|---|
| Delete **users** | |
| Delete a **channel** | |

Thanks to our CRUD brainstorm above, we can now further define services we need to build:

| Service | Corresponding API Endpoint |
|---|---|
| Videos | `/videos` |
| Users | `/users` |
| Comments | `/comments` |
| Recommendations | `/recommendations` |
| Search | `/search` |
| Channels | `/channels` |

## Tip: Demystifying Update in CRUD

The **c**reate, **r**ead, and **d**elete operations are mostly self-explanatory; however, **u**pdate can be misunderstood.

Most people agree that incrementing the "number of Tweet views" is an update. But there are less obvious updates such as:

- Liking a Tweet
- Replying to a Tweet

We wouldn't blame you if you thought liking or replying was a **c**reate operation. Likes and replies may be stored in different tables, and every new like and reply instance is a new field in the table.

However, the best practice is to have likes and replies stored in the Tweet table; it eliminates the cost of a `JOIN` operation. Therefore, a like or a reply is considered an update to the Tweet table.

Whether something is a create or update depends on how data is stored in the database.

To summarize:
- **Create:** Inserting a new row (`INSERT` command) in a table
- **Update:** Changing an existing row (`UPDATE` command)

One last tip: do not consider *deleting* content as an **u**pdate. Yes, one could make that argument, but using **d**elete will simply be less confusing to the interviewer!

## Describing the How

Defining *what* to build can feel intimidating, but it'll become manageable with practice. CRUD helps.

Additionally, anticipate system design questions before the interview and prepare. You'll save time (during the interview) and provide better responses.

The next step, describing *how* to build a service, is infinitely more challenging. Consider this: we can brainstorm that a house requires a kitchen. But we're intimidated by explaining *how* to build a kitchen. Why? Neither one of us has built a kitchen before.

So, here's the takeaway: you'll feel comfortable building a kitchen or a software system if you've seen someone else do it first.

So, if you don't know how to design services, here are our step-by-step tips on how you can begin to learn:

1. **Read the full-length examples**. Don't feel bad if service design feels foreign and unfamiliar. All beginners feel that way. We also won't insist that you attempt the full-length questions without looking at the answers. Those examples are meant to help gain familiarity, promote understanding, and inspire confidence.
2. **Research terminology**. Write down terms and concepts you don't understand. Then investigate what they mean.
3. **Try building services on your own**. Designing your first service feels intimidating, but nobody became better by only watching others do it. Jump in and practice! Then compare your attempts with others.
4. **Practice with partners**. Practicing on your own is a great start, but there's no feedback loop. Head over to Lewis' mock

interview community and find practice partners. To sign up, just search for "Lewis Lin Slack" on Google.
5. **Read engineering blogs.** Learning how others approach and solve real-world problems will strengthen our skills. Pick a few companies you admire, search for their engineering blogs, and start reading.

# Mistakes to Avoid When Designing Services

As you become more proficient at designing services, you'll want to avoid these SDI mistakes:

## Mistake #1: Not involving the interviewer

The SDI is a two-way conversation. Most interviewers won't like it if you don't let them participate. For instance, they'll get frustrated if you:

1. Focus on an area that they don't want to discuss.
2. Spend more time talking than necessary.
3. Make assumptions that don't make sense to them.

To counteract this, always check that the interviewer is comfortable with where you're headed. Here are some examples:

1. *Looks like there are three main services we should consider: orders, customers, and suppliers.* **Am I missing anything?**
2. *Of the three subsystems, the order subsystem is the trickiest to build, and here's why.* **Are you okay if I tackled that one first?**
3. *I'm going to estimate the storage we need for a YouTube-like service. My calculation will be based on the number of videos uploaded per user. Based on my experience, each user will upload one video per month.* **Is that in line with what you'd expect?**

You may have noticed that each one of the questions above can be answered with a simple yes or no. We call that a close-ended question. You may be wondering why we don't ask equivalent open-ended questions like:

1. *What services should we consider?*
2. *Which subsystem would you like me to start with?*

3. *How many videos will be uploaded each month?*

Many interviewers feel that open-ended questions get the interviewer to answer for the candidate. In other words, it feels like cheating.

But you never know. Some interviewers may be comfortable with open-ended questions. You're always welcome to try open-ended questions first. If it feels like the interviewer is hesitant to answer your open-ended questions, then fall back to providing your own assumptions or hypotheses and then confirming with the interview with a close-ended question.

## Mistake #2: Diving into the minutiae

We've seen many candidates dive too quickly into the details like video compression algorithms. Candidates do this because it's either the first thing that comes to mind or because it's their area of expertise.

Interviewers don't like it when candidates dive deep so quickly. Here's why:

1. **Disagree with your focus.** The interviewer would rather discuss another of the problem.
2. **Check your ability to see the big picture.** Are you familiar with all aspects of the problem? Or are you familiar with only one area?
3. **Test your ability to explain your priorities.** Why did you choose to focus on video compression? Why not focus on something else?

Counteract this bad habit by:

1. **Structure your answer** and start with the big picture. Here's an example: "When building a YouTube clone, five services come to mind: 1) videos, 2) users, 3) comments, 4) recommendations, 5) search, and 6) channels."
2. **Get their input.** E.g. "Of the six areas, is it okay if I focused on search?"

3. **Provide context.** E.g. "The reason I chose search is for these three reasons..."

## Mistake #3: Talking too long

Interviewers can't stand long-winded candidates. They want to cover more questions. They've got back-to-back meetings, and they can't afford to have the interview run long.

But the most important reason why they hate talkative candidates: they're impatient. Why tolerate those that fumble through a question or drone on about some unimportant detail? Interviewers dream of having more time to enjoy the Internet by dismissing candidates early.

Here are some tips to prevent yourself from talking too long:

### Set expectations early

Ask how long you should spend on a particular problem. E.g. "Did you want a 15-minute answer? Or a more detailed 60-minute answer?"

### Set the scope

Be clear on what you will and will not cover. E.g. "Okay, I can cover X, Y, and Z. But for the sake of time, I will leave out security concerns. Are you okay with that?"

### Pause to collect your thoughts

The typical candidate fills their response with filler words and phrases. Here's an example:

*Wow, that's a really good question building YouTube. I've never really thought about it... Let me think about that... Oh yeah, maybe we should build an upload and download video service... Oh, maybe a...*

As you can see from this example, the candidate injects filler phrases because he's trying to buy time to think. Don't torture the interviewer with your loquacity. Just ask for time to collect your thoughts, think silently on your own, and share your beautifully edited thoughts with the interviewer.

## Be RESTful: API Best Practices

REST is an important acronym. It stands for representational state transfer. REST is known for using the following HTTP commands to read and write data:

- `GET`
- `POST`
- `DELETE`
- `PUT`

Another concept we've touched on is API. An *API* is a way to communicate with a system. For instance, it's a common best practice for web and mobile clients to communicate with a back-end service via an API. Utilizing APIs makes software easier to code, manage, and understand.

An *API endpoint* is a location where a third party can make a *request* and receive a *response*.

For example, a developer can call the following Twitter endpoints:

| Twitter API Call | Description |
| --- | --- |
| `POST /statuses/update` | Write a Tweet (aka status update) |
| `GET /favorites/list` | Get a list of Tweets the user has liked |
| `POST /statuses/retweet/:ID` | Retweet a specific Tweet |

The most important thing about Twitter's well-designed API: it defines the key sub-components of the larger system.

We're not required to use the API endpoint naming convention when defining services. However, we strongly recommend that you do so, and here's why:

- It demonstrates your familiarity with RESTful APIs.
- It shows that you design with the Web in mind.

- It signals your willingness to build service-oriented architectures, which is an industry practice.
- Thinking in terms of APIs forces you to decompose a complicated system.

Defining the APIs, in step 3, structures your answer so it's easy to follow. It almost feels like a roadmap; the interviewer knows where you're headed and what you'll cover.

It shows you can do the job. Defining an API could be your job.

## API Tip #1: Use Nouns

There are many API best practices, but the most important one is to use nouns, not verbs.

In the real world, you'll see many API endpoints that start with verbs:

- `/PlayVideo`
- `/DeleteVideo`
- `/ShowComments`

These naming choices feel reasonable at first glance. However, some interviewers will cringe.

The reason: API endpoints are typically invoked via HTTP requests. And each HTTP request is accompanied by verbs such as GET, PUT, POST, and DELETE:

- GET refers to a *read* operation.
- PUT refers to an *update* operation.
- POST refers to a *create* operation.
- DELETE is self-explanatory.

As a result, it's a bit odd, naming-wise to invoke an API endpoint with two verbs like this:

`DELETE /ShowComments`

Moreover, this example is illogical. How can you *delete* and *show* comments at the same time?

It makes more intuitive sense to name endpoints as nouns like /Comments and apply the appropriate HTTP operation to each one like this:

```
POST /comments
GET /comments
PUT /comments
DELETE /comments
```

### API Tip #2: Use nesting to show the hierarchy

Here's an example of a well-nested API endpoint. It shows that many orders can be associated with a single user.

| Route | Description |
|---|---|
| /users | Returns a list of users |
| /users/1 | Returns a specific user with id = 1 |
| /users/1/orders | Returns orders for user with id =1 |
| /users/1/orders/2 | Return order id = 2 for user with id = 1 |

Use a maximum nesting depth of two, perhaps three, to maintain readable and compact URLs.

### API Tip #3: Use plural

Some practitioners prefer plural API endpoints vs. singular ones. Here's why:

- GET /users make clear that the response contains a collection of users
- GET /user could return a collection or a single user

### API Tip #4: Support filtering and pagination

A request for all Amazon orders will take a long time. Filtering and pagination minimize latency and waste.

### API Tip #5: Return JSON

RESTful APIs can return different formats including plain text, JSON, and XML. JSON is the industry standard today. It is considered fairly readable while being less verbose than XML. It's also faster to parse than XML.

# Chapter 6 Design the Service: Advanced Strategies

## Introducing Design Strategies

As you review the solution examples, you'll see recurring solutions. For example, many social media sites:

- *Proactively* **push** information to users rather than *reactively* waiting for users to **pull** the information
- Use a **main-replica** configuration to remove read bottlenecks
- Use a **denylist** to ban specific IP addresses from creating suspected misinformation accounts.

Push-pull, main-replica, and denylist are just a few strategies that software engineers, over the decades, have deduced as optimal, or at least commonly accepted, ways of solving recurring problems. We will call these "design strategies," and we've summarized the most important ones below.

Memorize them. They'll offer valuable guidance on what your solution needs to do.

One more thing, many of these design strategies go by many different names. We've selected the clearest and most memorable names.

## Design Strategies You Need to Know

### Information Processing Strategies

Here are the most common strategies to process a stream of information:

#### Batch Strategy

**Description**
The batch strategy, also known as scheduled processing, collects and delays the processing of jobs until a later date.

**Example**
Uploading a video is time-consuming and computationally intensive.

A website may choose to batch and process the videos during off-peak hours when there are more server resources available. Also, if the site performance does slow down, fewer users would see the impact during off-hours.

**Why Use It**
The main reason for batch processing is to conserve computing resources, especially in situations where the processing doesn't have to be immediate.

Another reason is to minimize the setup cost for each job. For example, processing one large file often requires less server and network resources (in aggregate) vs. processing millions of little files.

## Chain-of-Command Strategy

**Description**
The chain-of-command strategy processes information in a pre-defined sequence.

**Example 1**
A system's security service uses a chain-of-command pattern. For example, the service may start with:

1. Invoking a CAPTCHA service to prove a user is human
2. *Then* verifying that the username and password are correct
3. *Then* checking that the user is using an IP address specified on the allowlist
4. *Then* confirming that the user is logged in from a previously used browser
5. *Then* initiating a two-factor authentication service

**Example 2**
Help desk systems also utilize a chain-of-command pattern. For instance, help desk software may start by:

1. Providing an automated, self-serve response
2. THEN transferring a customer call to a tier 1 agent
3. THEN transferring the call to a tier 2 agent
4. THEN transferring the call to a tier 3 manager

**Why Use It**
The chain-of-command strategy enforces a sequence of services or checks.

**Note**
The chain-of-command strategy is very similar to a cascading set of if-then statements.

## Checklist Strategy

**Description**
The checklist strategy is a list of items that need to be done or to be considered.

**Example**
To display a newsfeed, the service must go through a user's checklist of friends. That is, for each friend, get the most recent updates.

Then display those results in aggregate, sorted by most recent first. Do not group the updates by friend.

**Why Use It**
The checklist strategy:

1. Forces a service to *execute the same operation* on every single item on the list.
2. Tells us *where* we are on the list.
3. Tells us *how many items are remaining*.

**Note**
The checklist strategy is very similar to a for loop.

## Rate Limiting Strategies

Here are the most common strategies to throttle incoming requests:

## Fixed Window Strategy

**Description**
Limit incoming requests to a fixed number per interval. For example, a payment API may have the following limits:

- 100,000 requests per day
- 5,000 operations per request

Once the interval has passed, the quota gets reset.

**Why Use It**
It's the simplest strategy to implement. There is no need to keep track of when a user's quota expires, since the quota expires at the same time for all users.

However, there can be spikes at the beginning and end of the intervals. A system would rather smooth out its system utilization.

## Sliding Window Strategy

**Description**
Same as the fixed window strategy, but rather than have a system-wide expiration, set a per-user expiration, on a rolling basis.

**Example**
For every user that comes in, set a user-specific quota based on request time.

So if a user requests quota at 10:50a, have their quota expire at 10:49a the next day, even though other users have a different expiration time.

**Why Use It**
Overcomes the spiky usage concerns of the fixed window strategy but incurs extra overhead and storage to implement.

## Token Bucket Strategy

**Description**
Add request tokens to a bucket at a defined rate.

When the user makes a request:

- Remove a token from the user's bucket and allow the request.
- If there are no tokens in the user's bucket, then reject the request.

Limit incoming requests to a fixed number per interval. For example, a payment API may have the following limits:

- 100,000 requests per day
- 5,000 operations per request

Once the interval has passed, the quota gets reset.

**Why Use It**
A token bucket strategy allows a burst in requests, as long as tokens are available.

## Leaky Bucket Strategy

**Description**
We can augment the token bucket strategy to process requests at a fixed rate, using a queue.

The leaky bucket strategy is also called the queue strategy.

**Why Use It**
A leaky bucket strategy can help systems that have output constraints such as available network bandwidth.

## Limiting Concurrent Requests Strategy

**Description**
As an addition to the previous strategies, add an extra provision to cap *concurrent* requests.

**Example**
An e-commerce platform can receive 50 requests at once but will only output at a rate of 2 requests per second.

**Why Use It**
Another tactic to further manage system load.

### Critical Requests Strategy

**Description**
As an addition to the previous strategies, add an extra provision to allow *critical* requests.

**Example**
The service only allows 100 requests concurrently.

For critical requests, the service also allows users to exceed the concurrent limits by utilizing a special allotment of an extra 20 requests per day.

The user can choose to use the special allotment for a recently rejected request.

**Why Use It**
A tactic to manage system load while maintaining user flexibility.

## Communication Strategies

Here are the most common strategies to share information with different systems:

### Middleman Strategy

**Description**
The middleman strategy uses an intermediary to facilitate communication from one service to another.

**Example**
Planes, near an airport, do not communicate directly with one another. That would be too complicated, error-prone, and confusing.

The planes would need awareness of aircraft in the area, negotiate a communication channel to share information, gather information from each plane, and so on.

Instead, an air traffic controller serves as the middleman to not only gather and share necessary information but also determine landing priorities.

**Why Use It**

The middleman strategy:

1. *Reduces redundant communication.*
2. *Minimizes confusion.* It clarifies which service has the most up-to-date information and which service coordinates other services.

## Town Crier Strategy
**Description**

Town crier strategy involves broadcasting information in a single agreed-upon location (aka a town square).

**Example 1**

Wired and wireless computers broadcast information to a single location: the Ethernet network. The computers observe all messages shared on the network. Each computer chooses to process only messages intended for it.

**Example 2**

Websites are published publicly on the Internet. Users view only websites they care about.

**Why Use It**

The town crier strategy reduces coordination costs. It takes effort to figure out which message belongs to whom. It can be less expensive to broadcast messages to everyone and just have the intended recipients look out for their messages.

## Asynchronous Strategy

**Description**
Synchronous communication is defined as communication happening at the same time. For instance, the receiver and sender are present in a phone call.

Asynchronous communication is the opposite; communication doesn't happen at the same time. For example, an email can be viewed at a different time from when it was sent. By doing so, email gives both the sender and receiver more flexibility as to when messages can be sent or received.

**Why Use It**
Flexibility.

Asynchronous processes save the user and computer from waiting. They can do something else while a task is finishing.

## Latency Strategies

Here are the most common strategies to reduce system latency:

### Main-Replica Strategy

**Definition**
Main-replica is a technique that allows a group of databases to communicate, coordinate, and control one another.

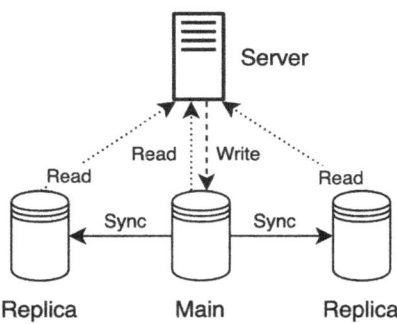

The main database receives all queries. It's connected to the replica databases. Each database is a copy of the main database.

When a program writes to the database, the main database receives that query. It then forwards that write to the replica databases to keep the information in sync.

When a program reads from the database, any of the servers can respond to the request. The replicas usually respond to reads; this frees up the main database for writes. As a result, the system can handle more database queries because multiple machines, not just one, are responding to the program.

This is a key advantage of the main replica pattern. In addition, if the main database fails, the replica databases can elect a single replica database to be the new main database. This election procedure ensures fault tolerance.

**Example**
In 1851, Charles Shepherd created a clock network. A grandfather clock served as the main clock. It would send electrical pulses to connected wall clocks to synchronize them.

**Why Use It**
Minimize user latency and increase fault tolerance by distributing requests across multiple devices or services.

## Push vs. Pull Strategy

**Description**
The push vs. pull strategy refers to two different ways information can be sent to users.

A pull strategy is a system design where users have to request information from the system. Based on the user's request, the system then reacts accordingly.

A push strategy is a system design where the system broadcasts information to the user proactively.

Put more simply, pull strategies are reactive while push strategies are proactive. Both push and pull strategies have pros and cons.

**Example 1: Push Strategy**
A news app knows a user will read every morning at 7 am. The system proactively pushes the latest news articles and images at 6 am. This saves the user from waiting.

**Example 2: Push Strategy**
A social media site chooses to display the first page of the app when all the images are ready. The system anticipates that the user will likely scroll to the second page, so it proactively loads the images for the second page in the background.

**Example 3: Pull Strategy**
A search engine indicates that there are over a million results for a popular search query. The system declines to give a more precise calculation unless the user requests it, conserving computing resources.

**Why Use It**
Pushing data proactively reduces latency but increases waste.

Forcing users to pull data minimizes waste but increases wait times.

## Precompute Strategy

**Description**
The precompute strategy involves *computing* (information) ahead of time. This minimizes wait.

This is different from the push strategy, which revolves around *transmitting* information before it's needed.

**Example 1**
A social media site chooses to precompute newsfeeds for users who follow more than 10,000 users. While this minimizes wait time for people who follow lots of folks, those users may not have the most recent results due to precomputation.

### Example 2
An airline reservation system considers billions of combinations when returning results for an origin-destination pair. This takes a long time. The system decides to precompute results, at the risk of showing routes and prices that might not be available when booking.

### Example 3
A social media site decides they want to show all users who have connected six degrees away from each user. This computation takes several minutes, even with powerful servers. The system decides to precompute results once a week to minimize user waiting.

### Why Use It
Minimize latency by doing high likelihood work beforehand.

## Lazy Loading Strategy

### What Is It
Load only the minimum or required parts of the page or application. Then load the remaining parts only if it's needed.

### Example
When displaying image results, a search engine chooses the show only the first page of results.

The search engine will only load the second page of results if the user scrolls to the bottom of the first page.

### Why Use It
Lazy loading's primary benefit is that it minimizes user wait times (aka application latency).

It also reduces the system's compute and network bandwidth costs.

## Peer-to-Peer Strategy

### What Is It
A direct connection between one peer to another without going through an intermediary third-party server.

In peer-to-peer networks, each peer can serve as both a client and a server, with its relationship changing over time.

**Examples**
- File-sharing networks
- Some video conferencing software

**Why Use It**
- Reduced cost
- Reduced latency
- More efficient use of resources

## Efficiency Strategies

Here are the most common strategies for systems to work (or process work) efficiently:

### Divide and Conquer Strategy

**Description**
Divide and conquer is a strategy that solves a big problem by breaking it down into smaller sub-problems.

**Example 1**
Instead of asking one computer, Google can ask several to find results to a user's search query. Google gathers each computer's sub results and then shows a single, unified result on the user's computer.

**Example 2**
A researcher wants to tabulate how often keywords appear in a very large file. The researcher wants to speed up processing time, so she writes a program that divides the large file into hundreds of small files. Computers map those words into counts. The computer puts counts for the same words together and then tabulates.

**Why Use It**
Performance.

After a big problem is reduced to several small problems, each small problem can be delegated to other computers and worked on in parallel, speeding up the process.

## Listener Strategy

**Description**
The listener strategy creates a role or service that receives notifications when a system's state changes. This role is called the listener.

**Example**
Rather than have its readers check for new articles every 15 minutes (aka polling), the Los Angeles Times can simply notify readers when a new article has been published.

**Why Use It**
Efficiency.

It requires effort to constantly poll for status changes. That effort could have second-order effects including wasted compute cycles and unnecessary power consumption.

# Space Reduction Strategies

Here is a common storage compression strategy:

## Mario and Luigi Strategy

**Definition**
The Mario and Luigi strategy saves space by saving only one instance of a shared component.

**Example 1**
A video game may have two characters who are near identical. The only difference is one is wearing a red shirt, and the other is wearing a green shirt.

Rather than waste space storing two near-identical images, store just one image and specify visual differences between each one. The computer can render the differences on its own without reading a second image.

**Example 2**
A dictionary service can store many words with the same prefix:

- ear (3 characters)
- earn (4)
- earls (5)
- earth (5)
- earnest (7)

To save space, a service can store a short version of the word by replacing "ear" with "1":

- 1 (1)
- 1n (2)
- 1ls (3)
- 1th (3)
- 1nest (4)

The system replaces the "1" with "ear" when displaying.

**Why Use It**
Save space.

# Synchronization Strategies

Here is a common strategy for systems to coordinate, especially write operations:

## Locks Strategy

**Definition**
To prevent multiple services from writing changes at the same time, a lock strategy forces a service to acquire the lock before writing changes. When one service has the write lock, other services cannot write. When that service is done writing, it releases the lock. Other services now have an opportunity to acquire the write lock.

**Example**
Online banking

**Why Use It**
Prevent overwriting data inadvertently

## Error Handling Strategies

Here is a common strategy for systems to handle system errors:

### Exponential Backoff Strategy

**Definition**
The exponential backoff strategy is a method for handling failed network requests. That is, a client retries an unsuccessful request by increasing the time between the requests.

This stops a failing service from creating a continuous negative feedback loop.

**Example**
1. A famous musician begins ticket sales at 10 am on a particular day.
2. At 10 am, thousands of users simultaneously make requests to Ticketmaster, a concert ticketing service.
3. If a request fails, instead of letting clients try again immediately, Ticketmaster makes them wait one second before retrying.
4. If the request fails, make them wait two seconds before retrying.
5. If the request fails, wait four seconds before retrying.
6. If the request fails, wait eight seconds before retrying.
7. And so on, until a predefined maximum.

**Why Use It**
Reduce server overload. This minimizes the number of requests a client can make in a given amount of time.

When a server receives too many requests at once, the server can overload and crash. Villains exploit this weakness by intentionally sending many requests, at once, to take down a server. This is called a denial of service (DoS) attack. Exponential backoff can help mitigate DoS attacks.

Exponential backoff can also mitigate cascading failures. Cascading failure happens when one crashing server can cause upstream servers to become overloaded. Those upstream servers can crash, bombarding further upstream servers with requests, and so on.

# Code Readability, Maintainability, and Elegance Strategies

Here are the most common strategies to make code easier to read and maintain:

## Wrapper Strategy

### Definition
The wrapper strategy is when a service encapsulates around another service. The new "wrapper" service inherits and usually extends the original service functionality without modifying the original's source code.

### Example 1
A third-party service provides inventory data in US Dollars. However, the data needs to be denominated in Euros. A developer can create a wrapper service that provides Euro-denominated data.

### Example 2
A developer wants to read, add, update, and delete information in a database (CRUD). To save the developer from worrying about the underlying database (vendor or database type such as SQL v. NoSQL), a wrapper service may be created to allow that developer to perform CRUD operations without understanding underlying database internals.

### Example 3
A video game gives its players a choice between three different races: Protoss, Terran, and Zerg. All three races perform the same actions:

1. Collect resources
2. Build structures
3. Build units
4. Attack

However, each race approaches actions differently. The developer could create a base race with the four different actions. The developer could then create a race-specific wrapper that modifies the base actions.

**Why Use It**
1. *Conversion.* Convert correctly from one format to another.
2. *Hide complexity.* Save users or other services from seeing and understanding the complexity of the underlying service.

## Paths Strategy

**Description**
The paths strategy provides multiple options when there are two or more paths a system can take to satisfy the user's goal.

**Example 1**
A user's goal is to get directions given a starting location and destination. A mapping application returns multiple paths including driving, walking, and public transit directions.

**Example 2**
A diner's goal is to order food from 9 pm to 12 pm. The restaurant server returns two menus the diner can order from: the dinner menu and the happy hour menu.

**Why Use It**
Elegance.

Using the paths strategy gives users choices to choose from without having to use different systems or services.

## MVC Strategy

**Definition**
The MVC (model-view-controller) strategy divides an application into three logical groupings:

- **Model** (Data Layer). Defines how the database is organized and manages the application's interaction with the database.

- **View** (Presentation or UI Layer). Handles how application output is rendered to the user.
- **Controller** (Business Logic Layer). Manipulates data input by the user.

**Why Use It**
Elegance.

Code that is written with the MVC strategy is easier to explain and follow.

It can also reduce development time by grouping related items together.

## Security Strategies

Here are the most common strategies to secure your system:

### Allowlist & Denylist Strategy

The allowlist strategy involves defining a list of entities that can communicate with a service, blocking others.

The denylist strategy is the opposite. That is, defining a list of entities that cannot communicate with a service, allowing others.

### Authentication Strategy

Authentication is the act of proving a user's (or system's) identity to a service. Authentication techniques are frequently applied during log-in. Common techniques include:

- Passwords
- Server certificates
- Fingerprint sensors
- Two-factor authentication
- Personal Identification Number (PIN Code)

### Auditing Strategy

A system can audit user access and activity over time. The system reveals recent activity to the user such as devices and locations where that user is logged in.

The user can then flag an activity that is suspicious or unauthorized.

## Authorization Strategy

Assign permissions to selected users or roles, usually through an access control list.

For example, the owner can remove accounts from the group, but normal users within the group cannot remove other accounts.

## Encryption & Decryption Strategy

Encryption is translating the text (aka plain text) into an indecipherable result.

Decryption is translating the indecipherable result into plain text.

The translation depends on a rule to translate plain text into its indecipherable output. This rule is often called a cipher. The cipher provides the mappings from input to output to facilitate encryption and decryption.

## Layering Strategy

A common tactic to increase security precautions by placing multiple security mechanisms before granting access.

For example, two-factor authentication is an example of layering two access methods – entering a password and then a PIN code from an SMS text – to increase system security.

## Proxy Strategy

**Definition**
The proxy strategy is to create a server or service that can perform actions as a trusted representative of another server or service.

**Example**
We may not trust a merchant to withdraw money directly from our bank accounts. But we may trust a credit card company to serve as a proxy and facilitate a debit transaction, which will eventually be debited from our bank account.

**Why Use It**

Security. Proxy services limit access to a valuable or sensitive resource. In software, proxy servers can provide services to users while masking your true server identity. This provides a layer of security for your system.

### Throttling Strategy

The throttling strategy involves slowing down an attacker by locking them out after reaching a threshold such as the number of failed login attempts.

### Validation Strategy

The validation strategy involves *checking before processing* a user's input.

Malicious users could embed executable code, such as JavaScript or database commands, to systems that do not properly validate user input.

## Practice Questions

Design an API for:

1. a hotel management system
2. a university course registration system
3. a social media platform
4. a coffee shop's mobile order software
5. a third-party payments platform
6. a sports news website

*Hint:* Think of the major components/objects within the system.

*See the Solutions chapter for answers.*

# Chapter 7 Articulate the Data Model

After you've defined the system components, the next natural step is to articulate your data model. This includes defining the:

1. Tables
2. Fields
3. Database options and other data storage

Additionally, some questions might ask you to define the file storage too.

## Tables

Let's start with the database tables. This is a simple mapping if you have your API endpoints well defined.

For example, let's say our video service has six primary API endpoints:

```
/videos
/users
/comments
/recommendations
/search
/channel
```

We can simply map each API endpoint to a table:

| Table Name |
|---|
| videos |
| users |
| comments |
| recommendations |
| search |
| channel |

### Tip when Defining Tables

The biggest fear when defining tables: what if I forgot a critical table? There are a few ways to protect yourself:

1. **Memorize.** Research and memorize popular data models for the most common system design questions.

2. **Draw workflow diagrams.** Diagrams can help you remember missing tables.
3. **Clarify with the interviewer.** You don't have enough time to discuss all the tables and fields. So ask the interviewer which ones they want.

## Fields

Next, define the table fields. This is another brainstorming exercise, so memorize common table fields.

Also, arguments and outputs of your endpoints can provide valuable clues for necessary table fields. As a quick example, let's say we have the following POST and GET methods for a /user endpoint:

### POST /user

| Purpose | Arguments | Return |
|---|---|---|
| Creating a user | Name<br>Birthday<br>Address<br>Etc. | User ID |

### GET /user

| Purpose | Arguments | Return |
|---|---|---|
| Retrieve user information | User ID | Name<br>Birthday<br>Address<br>Etc. |

You can see that the inputs and outputs of API endpoints hint at the relevant database fields.

## Database Storage

The table and field definitions are what we call the database schema or just schema for short.

Next, the interviewer will often ask about what database you'll use for your schema. The choice is often between SQL and NoSQL. Let's take a moment to understand the differences between the two.

## SQL Databases

A relational database is a database where the data points are related to one another.

The most popular relational databases are SQL databases. It's named SQL because SQL is the programming language used to insert, edit, and retrieve data from a SQL database.

To illustrate, let's say we store the following information in a relational database:

**Students Table**

| Student Name | Dorm ID* |
|---|---|
| Daniel Freeman | 1 |
| Fernanda Barbosa Cavalcanti | 2 |
| Zhen Hou | 3 |

**Dorm Table**

| Dorm ID* | Dorm Name* |
|---|---|
| 1 | Roble |
| 2 | Schiff |
| 3 | Alondra |

Because information is connected from one table to another, the relational database allows us to determine which dorm each student is assigned to by looking up the Dorm ID.

The advantage of a relational database is that it minimizes data duplication. Eliminating data duplication not only saves space but also (computing) effort to update the same information in multiple places.

SQL databases also have table fields and data types defined in advance. We call this a "structured" database. A structured database won't accept a new row of data if it doesn't meet the field and type requirements of that table.

Because they're structured and relational, SQL databases can efficiently search and retrieve multiple pieces of data at the same time by using JOINS to relate different kinds of data across multiple tables. For example, retrieving all orders for a given customer can be done in one fast query. If there are a lot of orders, the results can be requested one page at a time with pages after the first being delivered very quickly from cached results.

Popular SQL databases include MySQL and PostgreSQL.

## NoSQL Databases

NoSQL databases typically refer to non-relational databases. They're called NoSQL databases because non-relational databases do not use SQL as a query language.

The most recognized NoSQL database is the document store. Instead of tables, this specific NoSQL database stores each new data entry called a document, and related documents are grouped in a collection. Here's an example of a single document in a document store:

```
{
    "ID" : 1,
    "Name" : "Ananya Yogendra",
    "Email" : "ananya3030@gmail.com",
    "City" : "Delhi",
    "Country" : "India"
}
```

Popular NoSQL databases include MongoDB and Redis.

## The Main Difference Between SQL and NoSQL

You'll hear conflicting opinions about SQL and NoSQL. Some argue that NoSQL does not support transactions. Others say SQL is slower than NoSQL.

It's a never-ending debate. Both sides are right and wrong.

Both SQL and NoSQL have strengthened their respective shortcomings. So, if someone says SQL is fast or NoSQL does support transactions, they're arguably correct.

However, there is one distinction between the two that isn't controversial, and it's this: **NoSQL databases have a flexible or unstructured database schema**. This allows developers to store data without worrying about inflexible schemas or dealing with schema migrations.

NoSQL's biggest advantage, flexible schemas, is also its biggest flaw. Let's say you make a change to your NoSQL schema; any record created before that change will have NULL values in the new fields.

Developers will have to write additional code to handle these NULL values. Not only does this take time, but also creates a situation where unhandled exceptions can lead to buggy software. Given this drawback, many developers prefer SQL databases.

## How to Choose Between SQL and NoSQL

When designing the optimal storage solution, keep the following questions in mind:

- How much data will the DB need to support?
- How often is the DB going to be updating existing entries?
- Is this system particularly heavy in reads or writes?

A SQL database is often the best initial solution.

## Frequently Asked Questions: NoSQL vs. SQL

### Is NoSQL faster than SQL?

It depends.

SQL databases are generally faster for queries, joins, and updates. Why? SQL databases are normalized; the data is split into logical tables to avoid data redundancy and duplication.

NoSQL databases are generally faster for read and write operations because of their document-oriented nature.

### Is NoSQL better for big data applications?

Arguably, yes.

NoSQL databases generally write faster because they aren't constrained by ACID principles (atomicity, consistency, isolation, and durability). Given this belief, NoSQL databases have been very popular with applications with frequent writes such as log or leaderboard scoring data.

However, as modern NoSQL databases become ACID compliant, NoSQL's write speeds begin to slow, making it fair to say SQL could be as appropriate for big data applications as NoSQL.

## Non-Database Storage

Databases are adept at storing integers, strings, and floating-point numbers.

But what about files and other large content? Databases aren't ideal outside of primitive data types. Here are some additional storage solutions to consider:

Outside of primitives, databases don't extend well to other data types or binary files. To solve this issue, there are different solutions to consider.

### Distributed File Systems

File systems are used to store large binary files. You're probably familiar with file systems on your computer.

Open-source, distributed file systems, such as the Hadoop Distributed File System (HDFS), allow software services to store large amounts of data or media across multiple computers.

Distributed file systems also offer replication, which makes your system more fault-tolerant.

So how do developers use a distributed file system? Typically, the developer writes code that:

- Place the file in a distributed system like HDFS
- Then store the file path, as a string, within a database

One more thing, distributed file systems are most common for services with large files such as content streaming and media files. Not all services require a distributed file system.

## Object Storage

Object storage is another way to store large binary files. It holds files without a file system to govern where files are located. Developers can save a lot of time by not having to maintain a file system. The most popular object storage solution is Amazon Simple Storage Service or S3 for short.

To use an object storage solution, an engineer simply uploads data to a service like S3. Then S3 returns a unique ID. That data can then be requested using that ID.

There's another concept that's similar to object storage: block storage. There is one notable difference between the two: In block storage, a single large file is broken up into smaller chunks that are stored independently.

# Practice Questions

What tables and fields would you have for each one:

1. a social media site
2. an e-commerce website
3. an airline operations application
4. a ride-sharing application

*See the Solutions chapter for answers.*

# Chapter 8 List the Architectural Components

By the time you get here, you've already defined:

- Your solution works
- Clients communicate with your system
- Your system stores data

The fifth step in PEDALS is "L"isting the architectural components.

Congratulations! Only two more steps to go. And in our opinion, you've already completed the hardest parts of the interview.

## Introduction to Architecture

When it comes to architecture, there are three terms you should know:

- Logical architecture
- Physical architecture
- Cloud architecture

**Logical Architecture**

The logical architecture specifies how the system works without specifying the system's physical technology such as servers and databases.

Many would call the work we did in step 3, "D"esign the service, the logical architecture of a system.

**Physical Architecture**

The physical architecture specifies the underlying physical technologies and assets for a system. For example, our logical architecture might have a table named "Users," but in our physical architecture, we would specify that the "Users" table is running on Microsoft SQL Server on a Dell server.

**Cloud Architecture**

The cloud architecture specifies the cloud technologies and assets for a system. For instance, we might indicate that a system's images are stored on an "object storage service." Or if we want to be more specific, we can say that these images are stored on Amazon S3.

These days, most systems are built using cloud services like AWS. Few developers have to worry about the underlying physical technologies. Thus, during an SDI, when we say, "list the architectural components," what we typically mean is to define the cloud architecture. There's *no need to specify a scalable system at this point*; scaling out the architecture will be the next section of the framework.

So, what do you need to make your system *functional*? Often, the only necessary ingredients are a:

- *Server* to run your application code
- *Database* to store your data

You can draw a server and a database like this:

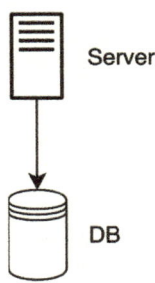

Beyond just these two elements, look into other components that may be essential to the design prompt. For example, your interviewer and you may have discussed security features to protect your system from attacks. In effect, you should attempt to include a reverse proxy server to mask your system's identity.

On the other hand, other system design interviews might include non-standard elements such as a trie. If that is the case, including an object-store instance, such as an Amazon S3 bucket, would be an essential system component.

Similar to these security and object store examples, different system design interviews may increase the minimum requirement for a functional system. It is essential to respond to these changes.

Examples of critical architectural components include:

- Compute: Servers
- Storage: Databases, object storage buckets
- Security: Reverse proxy servers

## Service-Oriented Architecture

During this segment of the interview, you may also choose to propose a more sophisticated system architecture that integrates service-oriented architecture. This system architecture style decomposes a single, monolithic system architecture into independent sub-components, each with a specific purpose.

If you and your interviewer have discussed the potential of SOA and its benefits to your specific design prompt, it may be beneficial to make design decisions based on SOA. This will not only allow you to stand out among many different candidates but also propose a more sound, compartmentalized system design. Proposing a service-oriented system architecture will give you more fine-grain control over scalability in your system.

**Benefits and Drawbacks of SOA**

| Benefits | Drawbacks |
|---|---|
| <ul><li>A compartmentalized approach to a large-scale design problem</li><li>A system architecture that more closely mirrors API</li><li>Can be scaled to address specific interviewer concerns</li></ul> | <ul><li>A complicated design may not be valuable in a compressed interview format</li><li>A poor explanation could lead to logical gaps between the candidate and interviewer</li></ul> |

## Architecture Verification

After proposing an initial system architecture, verify your solution with your interviewer to resolve any gaps in features or functionality. This review not only helps make sure you're on the right track but also helps you share your thought process with the interviewer.

Here are some things you can ask the interviewer:

- "Does the system fit the proposed API and data model?"
- "Aside from scalability, where can this system improve in supporting our platform workflow?"
- "Do you have any questions about this initial system architecture?"

To summarize:

- Think of this segment of the interview as a trip to a physical AWS store. You'll want to pick up everything you need to build a functional system that supports your expected feature set.
- Don't design your system with scaling in mind; address only functional problems.
- Review your simple, working solution with your interviewer at the end.

## Basics of System Architecture Diagrams

It's not enough to communicate your thoughts with words. Most interviewers expect you to write your ideas on the board, especially system architecture diagrams.

This is to your advantage. Most interviewers absorb information more quickly when they can see your ideas. Plus, there's something magical about the power of the pen. When you illustrate your ideas, you can be perceived as a thought leader.

So let's discuss how you can illustrate your architecture on a whiteboard.

### Standard Visuals

In this book, you will see symbols that represent different architectural components:

Browser

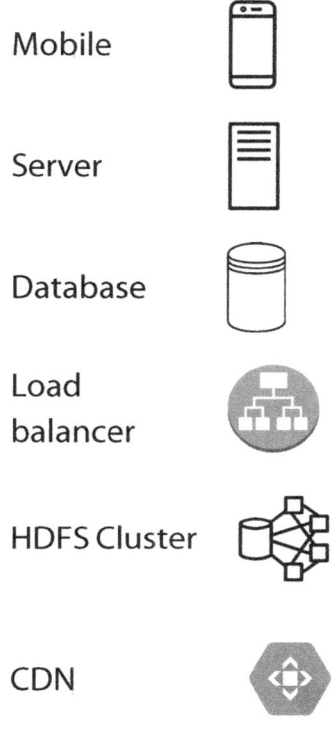

You'll notice that some of these icons are quite detailed, such as the load balancer. Your icons, during the interview, don't need to be this detailed. It's not a good use of your time.

Instead, we recommend your draw just servers and databases. Everything else you can represent with a clearly labeled rectangular box to save time.

## Architectural Generalizations

In more complex system design interviews, interviewers may ask for more sophisticated solutions. These solutions may push you to design compartmentalized, service-oriented system architectures.

With SOA, your system contains major subcomponents that interact heavily with each other. To better visualize this division of services, make your architecture more general. Think of your system architecture as essentially the interaction of major services rather than minor components. A common way to do this is to generalize your system to better highlight certain interactions.

Suppose we wanted to design Uber according to a service-oriented architecture. We could compose Uber from the following services:

- Client API
- User-Driver Matching
- Payments
- Notification

To visualize our system architecture, we should represent regions of our architecture based on services. This means that we visually organize our system at a higher level, as shown below.

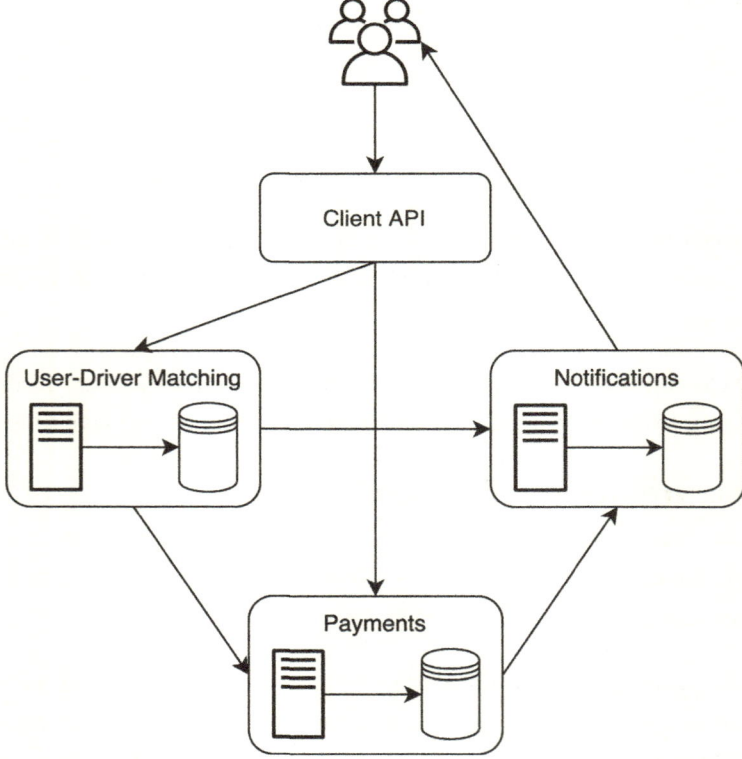

*The System Design Interview*

In the system architecture diagram above, you can see the boxed services of our general system architecture. This higher-level organization allows you to efficiently describe the system flow to your interviewer.

TIP: When drawing architecture diagrams, maintain a top down (or right to left) flow.

## Component Relationships

It's not enough to simply specify architectural components:

Draw a line between a server and a database to show that they're connected:

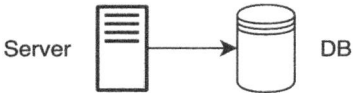

Add an arrow to indicate the beginning and the end. In the above example, the server (start) initiates the data request to the database (end).

# Chapter 9 Scale

## How to Tackle Common Scale Issues

Scale is the sixth and final component of the PEDALS framework.

Our system is nearly complete:

- In step 4, we designed the service.
- In step 5, we listed the architectural components.

Now, in step 6, we need to scale our architecture to meet the estimated scale requirements from step 2.

What were some of those estimated scale requirements? It included things like:

- Number of total users
- Number of active users
- Requests per second (RPS)
- Logins per seconds
- Storage needed

We're also looking to remove bottlenecks that limit overall system performance including:

- CPU
- Memory
- Storage
- Latency

To scale a small, functional system, we'll use some strategies you've heard before including:

- Load balancing
- Read replica databases
- Distributed file systems
- Content delivery networks
- Daemon process pre-computation

Below, we'll discuss how you can tackle some of the most common bottlenecks and scalability issues:

## Problem: Handling More Users and User Requests

Your initial architectural design may capably serve a small number of users.

However, it may struggle to fulfill the needs of a much larger user base. As more user requests come in, users will wait longer for your initial system to respond.

To handle this increased load, understand why your baseline system is struggling:

- You might have a single, under-powered application server.
- Your database may be underpowered too.

### Solution A: Horizontal Scaling & Load Balancer

Add more servers (horizontal scaling) and a load balancer.

Multiple servers increase the number of incoming requests that a system can handle in a given moment.

Having multiple servers is not enough. We need a single point of contact in front of those servers to direct traffic. This is where a load balancer comes in. It can redirect incoming client requests to the appropriate server, spreading the load.

Load balancers can have different rules for spreading out traffic on those servers. You'll find those details in the "Concepts You Should Know" chapter.

### Solution B: Vertical Scaling

Adding more memory or upgrading the CPU allows the server to handle more requests at a given time.

Compared to horizontal scaling, here are some advantages and disadvantages:

|  | Advantages | Disadvantages |
|---|---|---|
| Vertical Scaling | • An application can take advantage of vertical scaling without modification | • Can be expensive<br>• A single server creates a single point of failure<br>• Growth can be restricted after hitting CPU and memory limits |
| Horizontal Scaling | • Inexpensive relative to vertical scaling<br>• Multiple servers remove a single point of failure<br>• Potentially infinite scale and limitless growth | • Extra networking equipment may be needed, including load balancers, switches, and routers<br>• Application may need to be modified to work across multiple servers |

## Problem: Handling More Data Reads

Looking to decrease the read latency or increase read throughput? There are two solutions:

1. Read replicas
2. Sharding

### Solution A: Read Replicas

By adding read replica servers, your system can read important data concurrently, drastically reducing read latency.

How is this different from a single server? Well, a single SQL server may lock tables and rows, preventing simultaneous operations from accessing the data.

A read replica solves this issue by allowing concurrent reads on a separate or replica server. Replica servers increase overall availability too.

While read replicas provide many benefits, there is one major drawback: consistency. If users can tolerate the lack of data consistency, then a read replica can be a suitable choice.

## Solution B: Sharding

Sharding splits a single large database, typically residing on a single server, into smaller databases across multiple servers.

Here's why we shard databases:

Improved query performance. As a database grows, its query performance gets worse exponentially. That's because the database may have to search every row for the query's desired information. By sharding a database, queries go through fewer rows, leading to a faster response.

- Improved write performance. Rather than write to a single database, the system can write to multiple shards in parallel.
- Reduced cost. A single powerful server is costly. Sharding a database allows an organization to use inexpensive commodity servers.
- Increase availability. Other shards can continue if one shard becomes unavailable.
- Scale. A single database will have size limits. By sharding, a database can grow infinitely.

Sharding does have some disadvantages:

- Slower join performance. This is especially true if a process needs to pull data across multiple shards.
- Additional application code. Some database systems have sharding capabilities built-in. However, most sharding is implemented at the application level, which requires more system code.
- Recurring maintenance. Some shards can grow faster than others. If a single shard becomes significantly oversized, it will no longer provide sharding's benefits. As a result, developers will have to perform system maintenance and balance the shards by moving data from one to another.

There are different ways to shard your database. Here are some of the more common methods:

## Shard by Customer or Range

When picking up tickets at the box office, ticket windows can be split by the last name.

For example, ticket window number one serves customers with last names from A thru L. Ticket window number two serves customers with last names M thru Z.

Similarly, we can shard customers in the same way. That is, all customer records from A thru L belong to database number one, and so on.

## Shard by Geography

Sharding by geography puts system data, belonging to the same location, in the same shard.

Ride-sharing apps are ideal for geographic sharding. For example, Seattle's real-time supply and demand are most pertinent to drivers and riders in Seattle. As a result, we can shard real-time driver and rider by geographic region. That is, store all Seattle area data in a database that's in close geographic proximity to Seattle.

## Shard by Hash Function

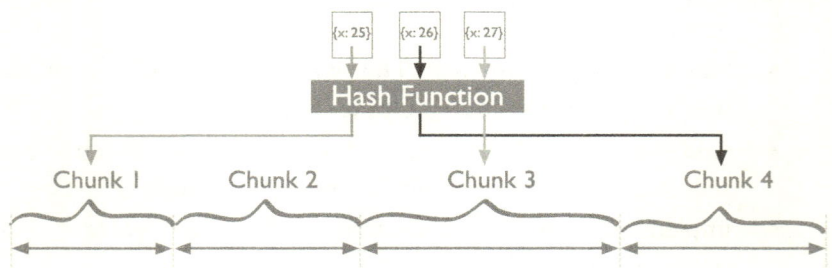

Screenshot / MongoDB

# Additional Solutions for Solving Scale Issues

## Problem: Avoiding Crashes

Your interviewer may ask if your system is fault-tolerant. That crash could be triggered by a corrupt database replica or a malfunctioning server region.

### Solution: Chaos Engineering

Chaos engineering is a discipline where engineering teams purposefully create controlled failure within a large-scale system.

Chaos engineering teams can emulate:

- Failure of a data center
- Failure of a database shard
- Randomly thrown exceptions
- Skew in distributed system clocks
- Failure of a key internal microservice
- "Storm" tests that emulate power outages in the system

When asked about potential system faults, we recommend that you:

1. Hypothesize what could break.
2. Explain how you could test your hypothesis.
3. Suggest how you would address the issue so that your application can run safely in both a developer and production environment.

Brainstorming is key. Make that list as complete as possible.

## Problem: Providing Data Consistency

Your interviewer may push for a solution that meets many heavy scalability requirements. By meeting these expectations, you may have to give up certain attributes of the CAP Theorem. For instance, as a system scales, consistency typically disappears first.

As a system scales, it's accepted that consistency continuously decreases. To meet increased consistency demands, we must review the CAP

Theorem: No system can simultaneously provide two of the following guarantees:

- Consistency – writes are immediately in effect
- Availability – requests receive a valid response
- Partition Tolerance – functionality despite network errors

When scaling a system, there is a direct relationship between consistency and availability. When horizontally scaling, you'll see availability dramatically increase; however, consistency will suffer because the system becomes distributed.

### Solution: Decrease System-Wide Data Replication
To create stronger read consistency, you'll have to decrease the effect of data replication your system creates, which will decrease availability. It's a tradeoff you should confirm with your interviewer before proceeding. This confirmation will not only let the interviewer know you understand technical systems and the CAP Theorem, but also that you can demonstrate sound workplace communication.

## Problem: Need to Improve Latency
After creating a large-scale, distributed system, your interviewer may bring up the concept of latency. As a system grows and creates an increasingly complex workflow, latency becomes a critical factor.

Like many other bottleneck issues, you may alleviate this issue through horizontal and vertical scaling. However, if you need additional strategies, you may consider caching.

### Solution: Caching
Caching can solve latency problems by decreasing response times and increasing system throughput.

Likewise, there are other, more niche solutions to poor latency that can be applied in different variants to improve system performance:

- Content Delivery Network (CDN)
- Pre-Computing expected requests with Daemon Services

CDNs allow large media content to be stored closer to users, decreasing the physical distance these large files have to travel to the end-user. This can lead to major latency leaps.

On the other hand, daemon processes can be extremely useful to pre-compute certain requests that are expected to arrive at a specific time range. Essentially, daemon processes front load computation before the request arrives at the system, which can be greatly effective if performed accurately.

# Identifying and Alleviating Scalability Bottlenecks

Although we have covered the common instances of scalability concerns, there are endless concerns your interviewer could bring up. To help you identify certain bottlenecks within your system, we are going to cover areas of a system you should examine to alleviate bottlenecks before your interviewer can bring them up.

During the "Estimate" segment of PEDALS, you and your interviewer communicated about the expected load your system may encounter. The information noted during that component of the interview is essential as it hints at what load the system should expect. It can help you appropriately provision scalability techniques to better craft a solution.

Take a look at the following areas of your system:

- Write and Read Compute Power
- Storage Capacity
- Latency Performance
- Data Availability/Replication
- System Consistency

These areas are the main components of a system that need attention during the scaling portion of the interview.

To understand how we can employ those previously listed scalability strategies, let's look at how a system grows as it accommodates more users.

Note: Our generalized recommendations are meant for illustrative purposes only. Scalability recommendations will vary from situation to situation.

## Less than 1,000 Users

An application server and a database are the minimum requirements for any system. This should suffice when the number of users is less than 1K.

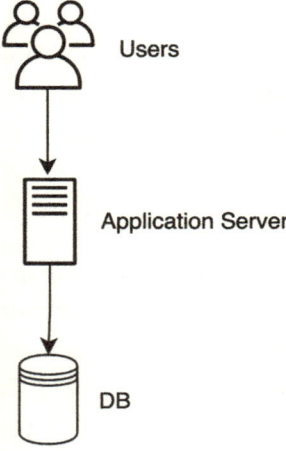

**Current Components**
- Application Server (aka compute)
- Database (aka storage)

# 1K to 10K Users

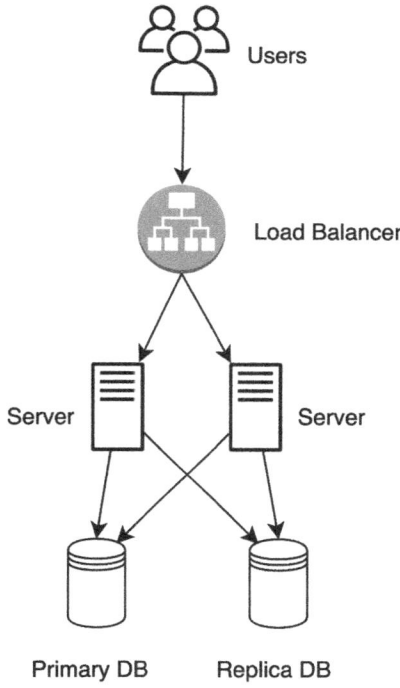

*The System Design Interview*

At this level, we'd recommend:

- **Additional application servers** to handle more RPS.
- **Load balancers** to direct requests to the application servers.
- **Database replicas** to increase availability, decrease latency, and remove a single point of failure (aka main-replica system).

**New Components**
- Load balancer
- Main-Replica database system

# 100K Users

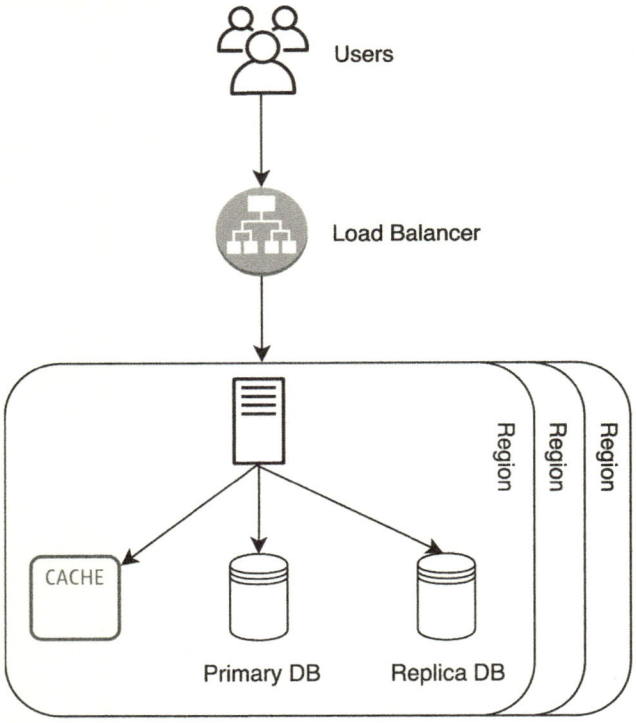

*The System Design Interview*

Around 100K users, we'd recommend different geographic regions such as the Americas, Europe, and Asia. The increased geographic proximity to our users will reduce latency. And the duplication of systems will increase capacity.

We'd also recommend adding a database cache. By caching results, we can minimize compute and wait times.

If you're wondering why we didn't consider a cache before implementing a main-replica database system, it's because a cache doesn't provide failover benefits that a main-replica system does.

**New Components**
- Regional systems

- Database cache

## 500K Users

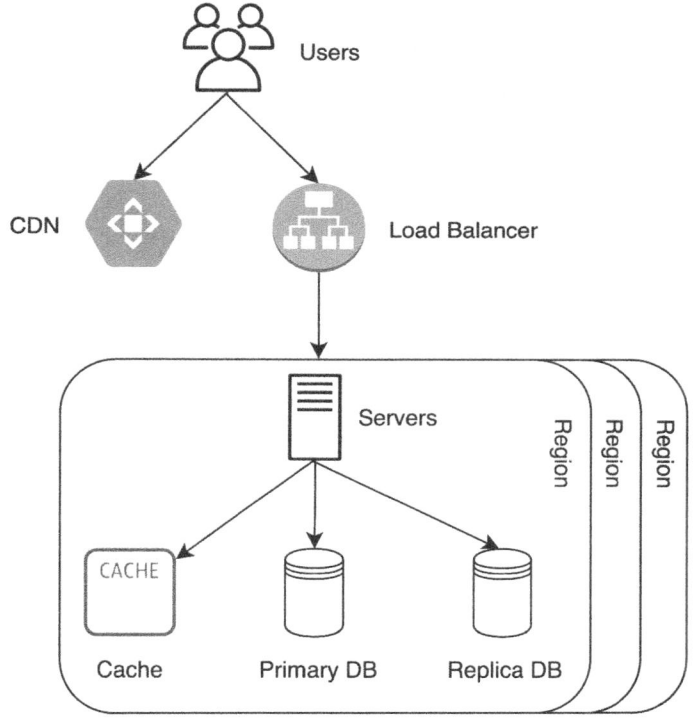

*The System Design Interview*

Around 500K users, we'd recommend using a content delivery network (CDN). CDNs are particularly ideal when an application delivers large media content files to users.

By storing large media files in geographic regions near users, it reduces the latency of sending those files.

**New Components**
- Content Delivery Network

## One Million Users

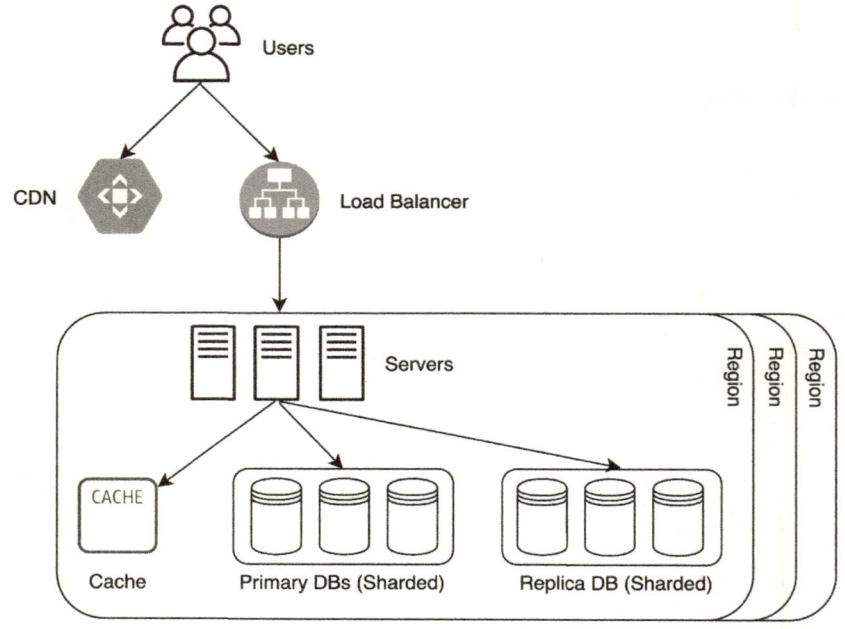

*The System Design Interview*

Lastly, as our system nears immense user base counts, we need to further divide our general user base to appropriate sizes. This divide and conquer strategy alleviates the burden of large data sizes. To do so, we can use tactics such as sharding to sub-divide our databases into clusters based on a function or method. In addition, we shard both main and replica databases to maintain a parallel data state.

**New Components**
- Auto-scaling regional clusters
- Sharded main and replica databases

Federation, which allows two or more systems to interoperate or share information, is another solution.

With these system scaling steps, you can see how certain strategies are employed at different levels of scale. More so than just scaling your system to meet user demands, your interviewer may introduce specific concerns about availability, consistency, etc. This interview is meant to understand a candidate's ability to *think fast* and *demonstrate their technical aptitude*.

To recap, here are our tips for building a scalable system:

- Start with a simple, functional system as your baseline. Then, scale as appropriate.
- Keep in mind the system requirements such as availability, consistency, and read optimization.
- Use strategies such as load balancers, horizontal scaling, and CDNs.

## Practice Questions

1. How would you address these scalability situations?
    a. Rapid user base growth
    b. Peak demand like Black Friday and New Years
    c. Users complaining about slow response times
2. Which sharding strategies minimize future work?

*See the Solutions chapter for answers.*

# Chapter 10 Example Cases

# Design Twitter

**Things to Consider**
- Use PEDALS
- Sharding can help scale the system, but don't forget about sharding's drawbacks.

**Common Mistakes**
- Unstructured approach.
- Not disguising one's use of PEDALS.

**Interviewer:** Let's design a simple, rudimentary version of Twitter.

## Step 1: Process requirements

**Candidate:** Okay, sounds good! In terms of requirements and scope, what does this version of Twitter support?

**Interviewer:** Let's assume a version where we have users who can follow each other, post Tweets, favorite Tweets, and generate their Timeline.

**Candidate:** To verify, the goal is to design a Twitter System that supports: Users, Tweets, Following/Followers, Favorite Tweets, and Timeline Generation?

**Interviewer:** Yes, that's correct.

**Candidate:** Can users retweet other Tweets or post images?

**Interviewer:** Let's assume, for now, users strictly Tweet text and hashtags.

## Step 2: Estimate

**Candidate:** Okay. In terms of load and capacity, do you know how many Tweets would be generated on a daily basis? And how many Timelines we would need to generate per day?

**Interviewer:** Let's say we have 100M users active on the platform that Tweets 1 to 2 times a day. However, on every app load, Twitter needs to generate the user's Timeline.

**Candidate:** We are supporting around 100M to 200M Tweets written per day. Also, since users' Timelines are generated on every app load, we must generate Timelines quickly. I would estimate, if the average user Tweets 1 to 2 times per day, each user opens the app around 4 to 5 times per day, creating 400 to 500M Timeline generation triggers per day. This is a system that would need to be more read-focused. Does this sound fair?

**Interviewer:** True, we need to be able to support quick Timeline views. To start rolling on this design, how would you approach this problem?

## Step 3: Design the service

**Candidate:** I want to establish some of the high-level concepts of the design, such as general API and system architecture, then dive into the details of scale and distributed system design.

I'm going to take these functional requirements and design a general API architecture that can drive the design for our system architecture and data model.

For the sake of a simple design in this context, let's say we already have a User ID and now need to support the features we discussed. For the API, the potential endpoints would be:

| Action | Endpoint | Endpoint Description |
| --- | --- | --- |
| Post a Tweet | /tweet | Takes the arguments of the userID that is posting the Tweet as well as the Tweet object itself through a POST request |
| Favorite a Tweet | /favorite | Receives a userID and a tweetID through a POST request to create a favorite link. On the other hand, removing a favorite from a tweet would come through a DELETE request. |
| Link users in our following/follower relationship | /follow | Takes the argument of the sourceUserID and the destinationUserID to create a relationship link through a POST request. |

|  |  | Conversely, a DELETE request would remove the follow relationship between those users. |
| --- | --- | --- |
| Display a timeline | /timeline | Takes in a userID and another argument lastCheckedTime that generates the user's timeline from that last time the user generated their Timeline till now with a GET request. |

**Interviewer:** Why did you choose these API endpoints? Do include your reasoning.

**Candidate:** These endpoints allow for a broad, yet specific, functionality to the API that encompasses the entire feature set we discussed.

Adding more fine-grained functionality would only lead to unnecessary complexity behind the solution. I'd say our API endpoints cover all the requirements.

**Interviewer:** I agree! I think the current API takes care of the feature set we have for the problem and has an appropriate design.

**Candidate:** Great! Moving away from API endpoints, I'd like to move on to the next component of design: System Architecture.

**Interviewer:** What do you believe is necessary for this problem in terms of system architecture?

## Step 4: Articulate the data model

**Candidate:** Given our current API, there is a clear client-server relationship that needs to be addressed, but I would like to look into how our servers would be able to handle such requests further than a single-server design. For example, we need to evaluate our data store to use a database management system, either SQL or NoSQL.

The data we would potentially need to store are Users, Following Relationships, Tweets, Favorites. By looking at the relationships between these different elements, a relational database, such as MySQL, maybe the better approach because of fast joins and searches when compared to a document-based database such as MongoDB.

It would be quicker to set up different tables such as:

- `USERS` that stores personal user information
- `FOLLOWINGS` that stores our following relationships
- `TWEETS` to store all global tweets.

We may even consider read replicas or even sharding, to speed up data access, as we scale.

**Interviewer:** That sounds good, I believe moving forward with a SQL database would be more appropriate in this context, although both approaches may be fair. What are some of your considerations for this architecture?

**Candidate:** I think discussing design specifics such as our Data Model as well as Data Flow would be more helpful as we grow our system.

Looking at the Data Model Relationship, we need to be able to solidify how we represent a User, Tweet, and Follower. Since we are using a SQL Database, we must be able to think about the problem mostly in terms of tables and joins.

Let's start off with our `USERS` Table. This table stores user information including userIDs, name, bio, and password.

| USERS | |
|---|---|
| uniqueID | INT |
| firstName | VARCHAR(15) |
| lastName | VARCHAR(15) |
| username | VARCHAR(15) |
| password | VARCHAR(15) |
| DOB | DATE |
| creationTime | DATE |
| currentStatus | VARCHAR(15) |
| bio | VARCHAR(150) |

*USERS Table Schema*

Moving forward to Following and Followers, let's have a table called `FOLLOWING`. The two columns in this table can be `sourceID` and `destinationID`, representing which user is following a certain user.

| FOLLOWING | |
|---|---|
| sourceID | INT |
| destinationID | INT |

*FOLLOWING Table Schema*

To represent Tweets, we have a table called `TWEETS` to be able to register all of the different global tweets from all users. Since Tweets are just text, we can store them directly within the database. If users can retweet and tweet non-text content, we would need to create a separate abstraction to handle storage.

| TWEETS | |
|---|---|
| tweetID | INT |
| userID | INT |
| content | VARCHAR(280) |
| datePosted | DATE |

*TWEETS Table Schema*

Lastly, to represent our favorites, we have a `FAVORITE` table that takes the userID that performed the action on a specific tweetID alongside the timestamp of when the action occurred.

| FAVORITES | |
|---|---|
| userID | INT |
| tweetID | INT |
| dateFavorited | DATE |

*FAVORITES Table Schema*

**Interviewer:** What you have represented is the Database Schemas, correct? How would you access a user's tweets or the number of followers a certain user has?

**Candidate:** Given a userID, we can filter the `TWEETS` Table on that userID key to retrieve that data. Likewise, on the `FOLLOWING` table, we can run the SQL command `COUNT` and filter destinationID to be the userID of interest to find the number of followers that the user has.

## Step 5: List the architectural components

**Candidate:** Having a scalable design would be an important attribute for any system. Additionally, having a maintainable system is crucial on the engineering side.

To be scale-aware, let's start off with 2 servers that directly respond to client requests and are fronted by a load-balancer. This load balancer will direct traffic appropriately to the most open server using a heuristic such as the number of active connections the server has. The load balancer will help us efficiently scale later as we get more users.

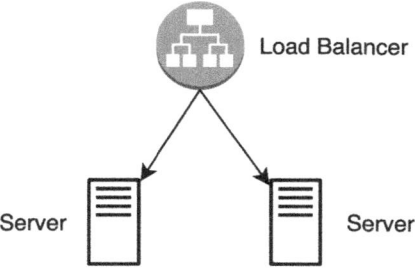

From here, let's add a single Database to store User data. We have a single SQL server that has multiple tables we discussed before.

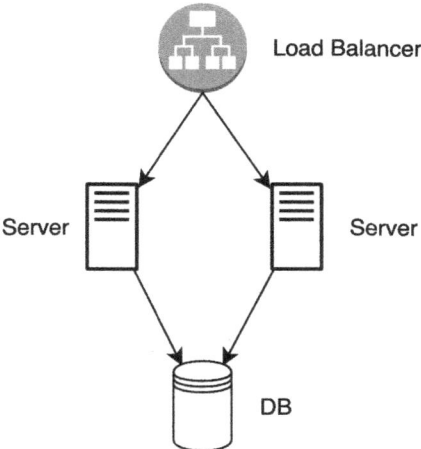

**Interviewer:** This looks like a good, basic system design. However, we have not tackled the design specifics nor scalability. Which of these would be an appropriate step to take first?

## Step 6: Scale

**Interviewer:** Looks good! Okay, now that you have the Data Model schemas out of the way, we know exactly how the data would look in our Database. In turn, let's assume we have millions of users now on Twitter and our service is slowing down. How can we tweak our solution to handle millions of users?

**Candidate:** To handle scaling issues, we can horizontally scale our servers behind the load balancer to handle more requests per second. However, even with a load balancer, we are bottlenecked at our database, since we only have one database server to rely on. This limits our throughput since we are relying on a single, critical database server.

To address this, we can increase throughout by sharding our database. To start off, let's place each SQL Table in its own server. Then, let's split up our USERS database into four different servers on a partition using userID. Specifically, every fourth user to Twitter will be placed in the same USERS database server.

**Interviewer:** How would you do that?

**Candidate:** We can use modular arithmetic as well as incremental userID to place people in different servers. Here's an example:

- *userID = 0 → 0 % 4 = 0 → DB #0*
- *userID = 1 → 1 % 4 = 1 → DB #1*
- *userID = 2 → 2 % 4 = 2 → DB #2*
- *userID = 3 → 3 % 4 = 3 → DB #3*
- *userID = 4 → 4 % 4 = 0 → DB #0*
- *... and so on*

In addition to our USERS database, we can shard our TWEETS database too.

**Interview:** Do you see any gaps with sharding?

**Candidate:** I do. The `FOLLOWING` table comes to mind.

Let's say a row in that table has userID 23 (sourceID) following userID 26 (destinationID):

- userID : 23 → 23 % 4 = 3 → Shard #3
- userID : 26 → 26 % 4 = 2 → Shard #2

To retrieve information about user 23 and 26, the system would access both shards 2 and 3. That could introduce unnecessary latency.

To alleviate latency, we can duplicate that data in shards 2 and 3. The downside is that our `FOLLOWING` data will be double the size.

We'll also want to shard our `FAVORITES` table appropriately. The most common scenario is to see all the favorites for a single user, so we should put the user's favorite Tweets on the same shard rather than scattering them across shards.

**Interviewer:** I like your sharding solution. So, what does the current system architecture look like right now?

**Candidate:** As of now, we have our load balancer masking our horizontally scaled servers. Behind these servers is a database system sharded by `userID` or `tweetID` to allow for multiple read/write operations simultaneously. In fact, we can extend our sharding system to 8+ shards to increase throughput. However, for our current scaling demand, let's leave it at 4 shards.

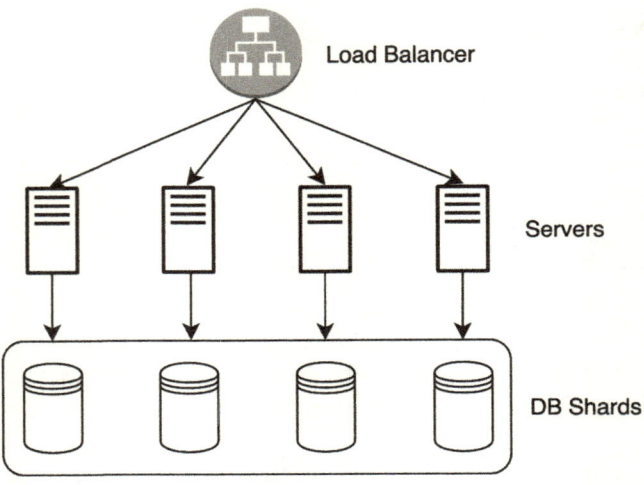

*All four Shards contain all tables mentioned above*

*The System Design Interview*

To make our system more robust, we need to create a more decentralized system and protect against failovers. To solve this issue, I believe we need to solve our read-write problem. All of these database servers are responsible for reads and writes and following a standard 80-20 rule for reads-writes, we should convert each of these servers into main-replica relationships.

**Interviewer:** Could you explain more? How would you go about splitting the workflows and optimizing reads?

**Candidate:** Take each shard and convert it into a small cluster: a single write server followed by 2 or more read clusters that provide more availability to users. Although this may lead to some inconsistencies in the data, missing one Tweet in a Timeline snapshot would not create client-side issues. We are losing some consistency between database servers in order to gain a great increase in availability to users.

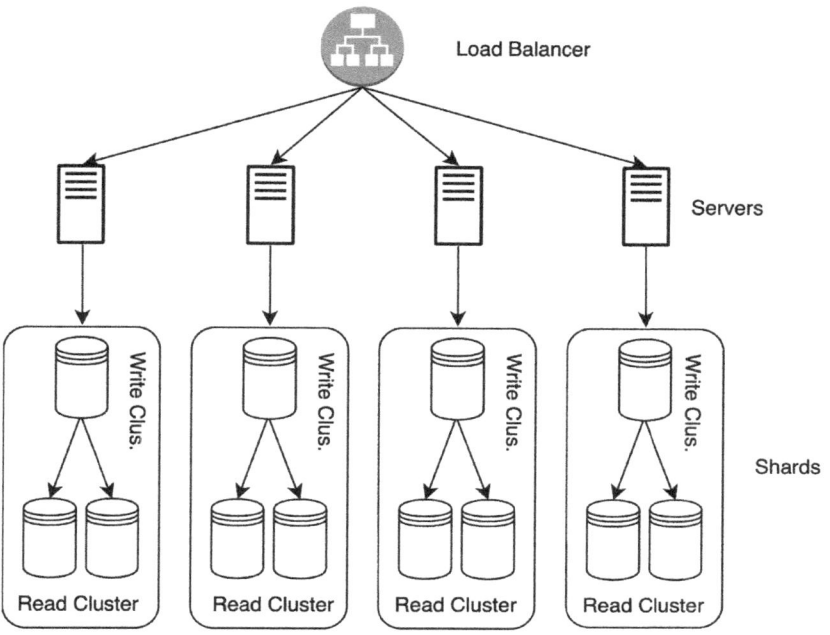

*The System Design Interview*

With this design, read requests will directly flow to replica servers, where response time is faster and multiple accesses can be delivered simultaneously. From the main-replica relationship, we have a much faster system that produces a higher throughput.

The current layout has the same workflow for reads and writes. But that doesn't make any sense; we're assuming most of the requests to be reads. We can separate our read and write workflows so that they are:

1. Independent
2. Optimized

To design these independent workflows, let's look at the API designed earlier:

- `/tweet`
- `/favorite`
- `/follow`
- `/timeline`

/*timeline* is the most interesting because the user never writes to the timeline. It's always a read request. So, we can create a new read-optimized workflow for that API endpoint.

Here's what a new read-optimized workflow would look like: it would route those requests to our read-only database servers. This avoids concurrency issues within our system.

Write requests are routed to write-only servers. These write-only servers will replicate their changes and modifications to the read-only servers.

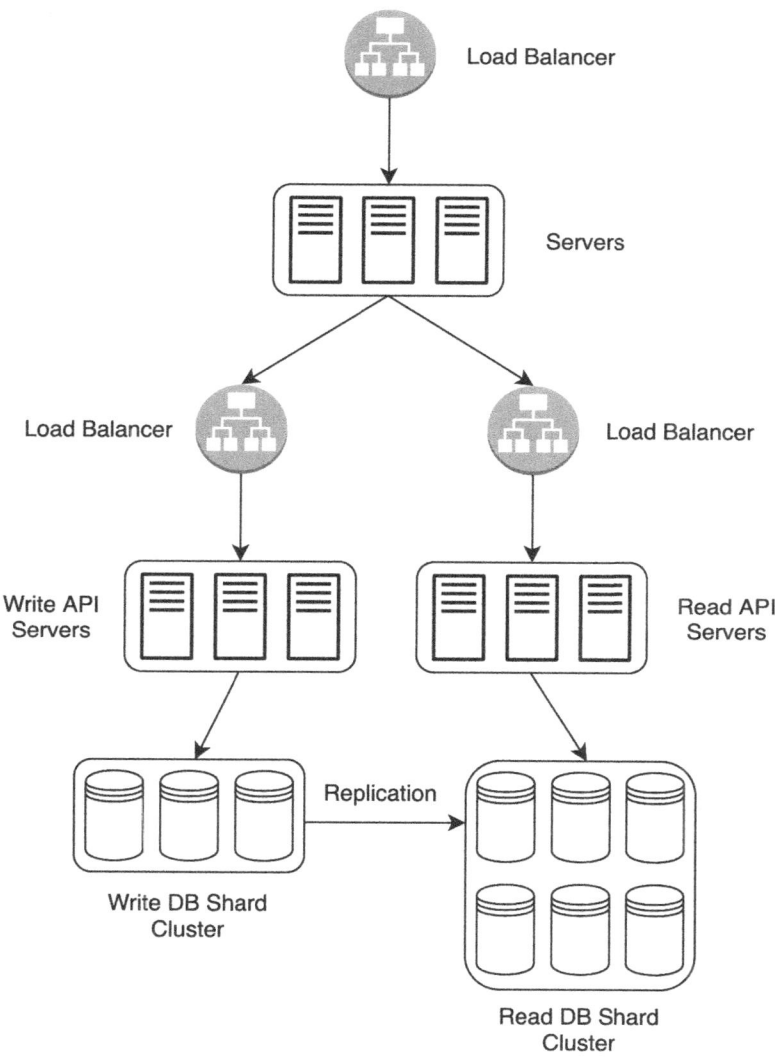

*The System Design Interview*

**Interviewer:** I like this incremental improvement. What do you think would happen, with your current design, if demand is higher than expected?

**Candidate:** This solution is horizontally scalable. That is, we can easily add more servers to handle more requests on both the read and write sides.

On the database side, if we added database servers, we would have to reshard. Based on the user growth at that point, we'll have to come up with a better rule to have balanced and optimized database servers. Would you like me to dig into those details?

**Interviewer:** That's a very pragmatic response. There's no need to do that. I think we're all set for now. Thank you for your answer.

# Design Instagram

**Things to Consider**
- How can you ensure user passwords are not susceptible to theft?
- Pay attention to storage mechanics.

**Mistakes to Avoid**
- Not adjusting PEDALS to the situation

**Interviewer:** I want you to design Instagram.

## Step 1: Process requirements

**Candidate:** Sure. Can you tell me more?

**Interviewer:** The goal is to design a system where users can share images with a caption and also consume an image feed from other users they follow.

**Candidate:** Are we supporting all of Instagram's current features such as Explore, Activity, and Feed?

**Interviewer:** For this problem, let's just look at the heart of the application. Your answer should define a system that can:

- Create accounts
- Post images
- Generate user feeds
- Search for images, based on captions or location

**Candidate:** Yep! That makes sense; I can design a system around those requirements. What kind of load should the application support?

## Step 2: Estimate

**Interviewer:** Why does that matter?

**Candidate:** It'll help us determine how to scale the system. I'm looking specifically for estimates on users, posts, and CPU consumption.

**Interviewer:** Okay. For users, let's say we have around 50M users and rapidly growing. Each user posts one image every one to two weeks. As for other numbers, we'll cross that bridge when we get there.

**Candidate:** Okay. I'll plan on supporting the current 50M users with some room to handle the increased load.

**Interviewer:** Sounds good.

**Candidate:** The requirements are fairly clear, so let's start by designing the service by fleshing out the API. From there, we'll talk about system workflow, the data model, our basic cloud architecture, and then finally scale that architecture to support our load requirements. Sound good?

**Interviewer:** Go for it.

## Step 3: Design the service

**Candidate:** First, let's open an endpoint labeled `/account` that takes in the initial personal information of this user. This route can be used through the many different HTTP verbs. For example, creating an account will be done through a POST request. On the other hand, retrieving information about an account will be conducted through a GET request with the appropriate user id.

To post an image, let's say client devices interact with another route called `/content`, which accepts data such as the image, caption, and location for a single post with a POST request. Let's call it 'content' so it supports additional types of media in the future.

When the app loads, just like Instagram, let's trigger a GET request to `/feed` which aggregates and displays the user's feed. For input, I believe we only need the userID.

Perhaps another input parameter could be the last time the user was active. We can generate the feed more efficiently by only showing new feed items.

Lastly, we can open the last endpoint labeled /search that accepts a search term with a GET request.

These are all of the key endpoints that I can think of at the moment. Did I miss any?

**Interviewer:** This looks like a strong start. We can discuss additional API endpoints later if need be.

## Step 4: Articulate the data model

**Candidate:** Alright. Next, let's create the data model.

**Interviewer:** What considerations should we have for our data store?

**Candidate:** The first question: what kind of database should we use? I'd recommend a relational database such as PostgreSQL. We have relational data that fits well with SQL's table format. SQL can also support sharding too.

**Interviewer:** No disagreement here. What's next?

**Candidate:** Defining the database schema. Let's start with the USERS table. It'll store the following:

| USERS | |
|---|---|
| uniqueID | INT |
| firstName | VARCHAR(15) |
| lastName | VARCHAR(15) |
| username | VARCHAR(15) |
| password | VARCHAR(15) |
| DOB | DATE |
| creationTime | DATE |
| currentStatus | VARCHAR(15) |
| bio | VARCHAR(150) |

*USERS Table Schema*

Next, let's define a FOLLOWING table that stores the relationships between users. In this table, the server should support a sourceID and a destinationID in each row to represent the following relationship.

| FOLLOWING |
|---|

| | |
|---|---|
| sourceID | INT |
| destinationID | INT |

*FOLLOWING Table Schema*

Lastly, we need a POSTS table:

| POSTS | |
|---|---|
| postID | INT |
| userID | INT |
| storagePath | VARCHAR (256) |
| timestamp | DATE |
| Location | STRING |

*POSTS Table Schema*

**Interviewer:** Got it. Where do we store the photos?

**Candidate:** Not a database. A file storage system would be more appropriate. The database can then store, in a string, the file location of a photo.

I'd recommend using a Hadoop Distributed File System (HDFS). HDFS allows for a single main node that knows where files are located on multiple replica nodes as well as their copies.

**Interviewer:** Doesn't HDFS only contain one main node? Won't this be a major system vulnerability?

**Candidate:** That is correct. To mitigate the single point of failure, we can create a passive main node. This feature came with Hadoop 2.0.

**Interviewer:** That is a better approach. So how do we tie this all together?

**Candidate:** We've defined the API endpoints and database schema. Did you need me to draw a service workflow?

**Interviewer:** That's not necessary. I'd like you to move onto the cloud architecture.

## Step 5: List the architectural components

**Candidate:** Okay, let me sketch the cloud architecture.

*The candidate draws the following*

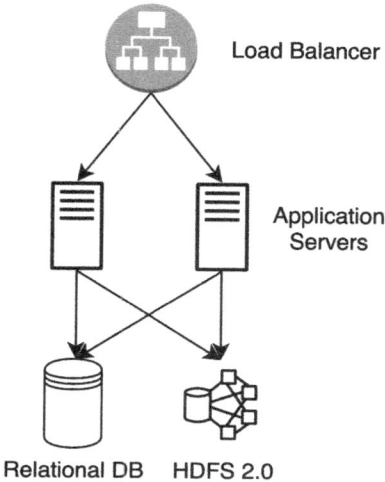

So, we have an application server layer. In front, we have load balancers to maximize throughput. Behind the application servers, we have our database and our HDFS system.

**Interviewer:** Walk me through the workflow when a user posts an image.

**Candidate:** Sure, I can explain. Let's say the user posts an image:

1. The client device sends a POST request to /content.
2. The request flows through our load balancer (LB). The LB selects an appropriate server to execute the user's request.
3. The server stores the content to HDFS. HDFS returns a file descriptor. This file descriptor is used to locate the content later.
4. We create a new row in our POSTS table with that file descriptor along with the appropriate metadata.

We repeat this process every time a user posts an image or video.

**Interviewer:** Good. What would the workflow look like for a user who wanted to retrieve their Instagram Feed?

**Candidate:** It would look like this:

1. The client sends a GET request to the /feed endpoint.
2. The load balancer forwards the request to a free server for execution.
3. The server then queries our database server. We will retrieve the list of users that the person follows.
4. Next, we filter our posts for an ordered list of posts from users in their user list. To minimize waste, we can limit retrieval to only new posts since the last time the user generated the feed.
5. This provides not only the posts but also the file paths and metadata.
6. The client can now send requests for images and videos for the feed.

And one last suggestion: I'd recommend lazy loading the feed content to minimize client wait time.

## Step 6: Scale

**Interviewer:** Everything so far makes sense. Your application is functional, and I like your lazy loading suggestion. Let's discuss scale now: how can we make this platform faster and handle increased loads?

**Candidate:** Sure, I'll talk about decreasing latency first and then increasing capacity.

Right now, our system architecture is monolithic. This means every call is executed by any server. It doesn't allow us to utilize caching or any read optimizations.

Our system should transform towards a more micro-service architecture. That is, different servers should be responsible for different operations.

For instance, we can increase our throughput by dividing and optimizing our workflows for reads and writes. That is, we want to establish a main-replica relationship between our databases. It will increase our system availability. Reads will operate on a separate server and in parallel.

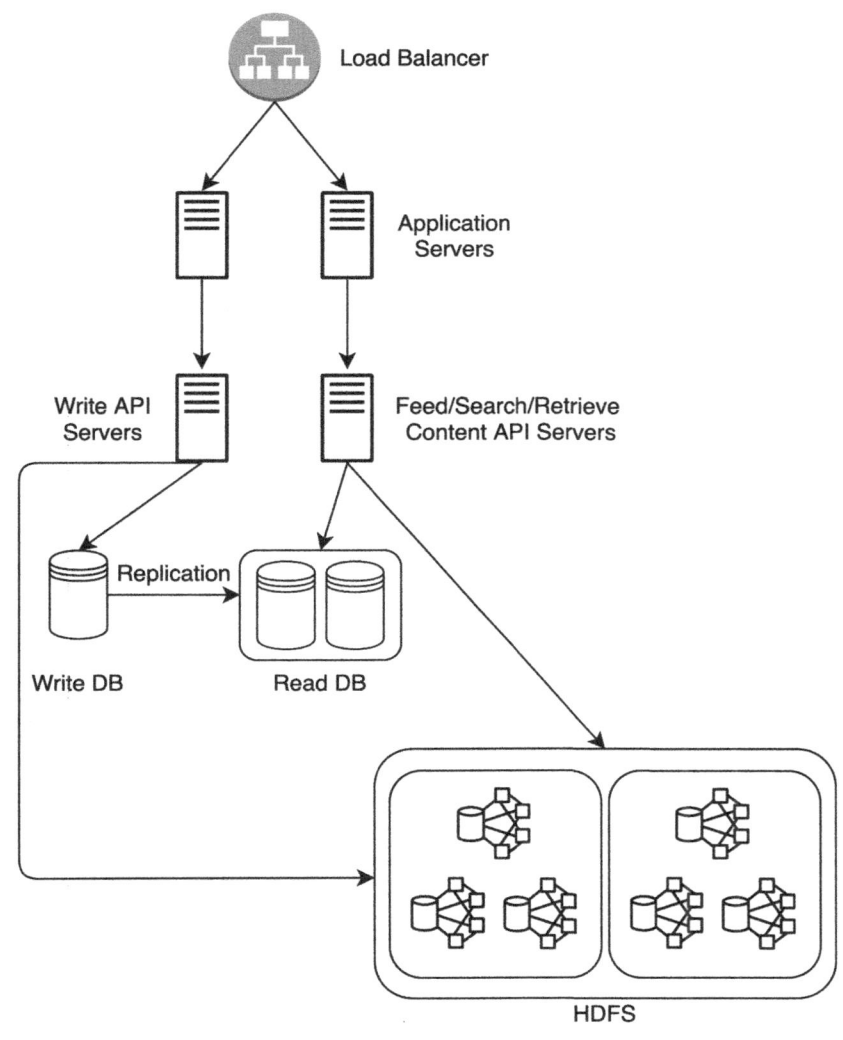

*The System Design Interview*

**Interviewer:** This makes the system faster and more robust. What other changes can we make?

**Candidate:** The first thing that comes to mind is horizontal scaling. It's less expensive than upgrading our existing servers, like improving the CPU and memory.

To do so, we mask each of our workflows, both reads and writes, with additional application servers and a load balancer.

For the load balancers, we can choose from different heuristics such as round-robin or least active connections.

**Interviewer:** What else?

**Candidate**: We can also dynamically partition the data.

We can cluster our database servers so that we have batches of around 4M to 5M users per cluster. We can spin up more database clusters as our user count grows.

From time to time, we'll have to adjust our partitioning methodology because our partitions may become imbalanced.

**Interviewer**: Why would the partitions become imbalanced?

**Candidate:** We may partition based on user characteristics and behaviors. Over time, characteristics and behaviors could change, leading to unbalanced clusters.

**Interviewer:** Do you have an example?

**Candidate:** Let's say 90% of the users are from the United States. As a result, we dedicate 90% of our database clusters, located in US regions, to US customers. Over time, maybe our mix of US customers goes down to 20%. It wouldn't make sense to reserve and keep 90% of our database clusters in the US at that point.

**Interviewer:** Thank you. Any other ideas to improve scale?

**Candidate:** Yes! Our platform is heavily read-dependent. Every app load requires a refresh of the user's feed and will require low latencies. In response, pre-computed user feeds should be stored because filtering and computing feeds will linearly increase in time as we increase our user base. We can create a new data store for pre-computed feeds to decrease response time on app load.

To pre-compute user feeds, a server-side daemon service can periodically compute user feeds that are later stored, waiting for the user API GET request to /feed.

This newly scaled design optimizes reads for Instagram, as most of our API calls will be to generate user Feeds and retrieve content from our HDFS. I believe this system is performant in scale and allows for dynamic growth with an increasing consumer base.

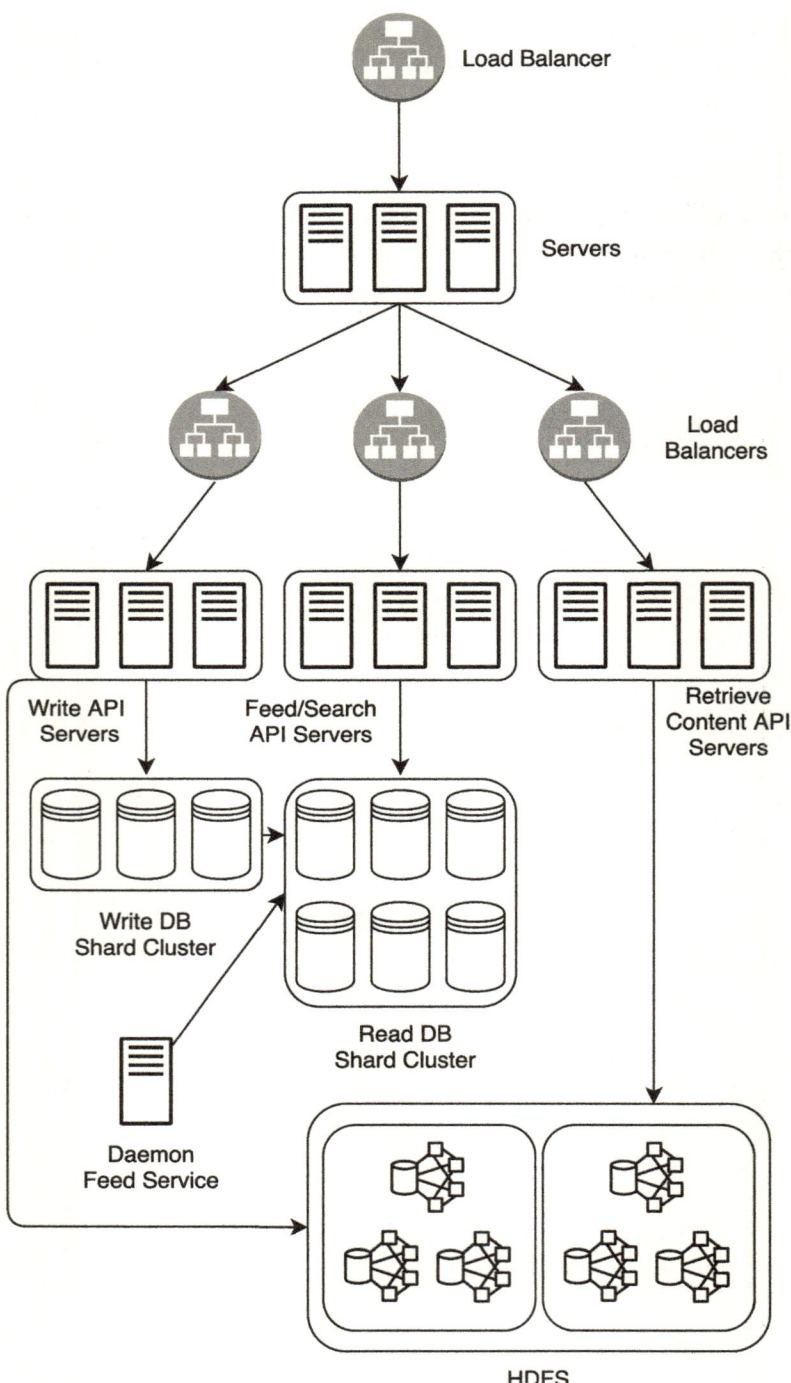

## The System Design Interview

**Interviewer:** Thank you! This solution addresses the latency we need for reads, the ability to scale as our user base grows and decentralizes the system for easier maintenance.

Even with this solution, I wanted to address a different perspective on this problem.

**Candidate:** Yes, of course! What other perspective did you have in mind?

**Interviewer:** Well, you addressed the scalability and latency requirements for this design prompt. On the other hand, we haven't discussed the users' security, especially their data.

If you were told to make this system robust in terms of security, what are two simple ways to protect this system?

**Candidate:** All right. I can see that this system may lack security measures to protect user data.

From a security perspective, I think we let through one major flaw through our design process: passwords.

Earlier, we designed a USERS table to store user-related information such as username, date of birth, and passwords. These passwords weren't encrypted. Instead, they were stored in plain text.

To address this issue, I believe we can establish an encryption algorithm with a specific rule to prevent plain text exposures of user passwords.

**Interviewer:** That's a good fix. Many systems that have sensitive user information encrypt their data. Can you think of other ways we could establish security measures for our system? To give you an idea, focus on a strategy that can prevent users from knowing the exact location of our server.

**Candidate:** One way we can cloak our system is through a reverse proxy. This places a server in front of our servers that receives all of the incoming request traffic. Then, the reverse proxy server forwards the message to our application servers for computation.

A reverse proxy server acts similarly to a load balancer. So, we can replace our load balancer with a reverse proxy server that redirects traffic just like our current system.

**Interviewer**: Perfect! Now your system not only protects user data, but also hides his exact IP address from other users. This will prevent further cyber attacks on our system in the future. Good job!

**Candidate**: Thank you! Did you have any other questions about the system or my thought process?

**Interviewer**: No further questions. This security follow-up was the most important one I had for this question. I appreciate your time.

# Design TinyURL

**Things to Consider**
- Hashing algorithms
- Bits

**Mistakes to Avoid**
- Don't overcomplicate this problem - think easy and fast

**Interviewer:** Good afternoon! Today, I wanted to work with you to build a system that behaves similar to TinyURL and Bitly. Are you familiar with them?

## Step 1: Process requirements

**Candidate:** Thanks for the welcome. Yes, I'm familiar with them. They take a URL, as input. Then it returns a short, concise URL. When the short URL is entered into a browser, the TinyURL service redirects it to the long URL.

**Interviewer:** That's exactly what we want to build.

**Candidate:** I do know that some of these services allow custom domains. For example, amazon.com/long-url will be shortened to amzn.to/short. From a branding perspective, amzn.to is better than bit.ly/short.

Do you want me to support custom domains?

**Interviewer:** No, let's keep that feature out.

**Candidate:** Okay.

So, let's say the user puts the URL "veryyyyylongurl.com/example-long-extension" into our system. Our system returns an N-digit URL with characters between certain bounds. The number "N" is for you to decide. As for the character set in this example, let's say the bounds are lowercase 'a' to lowercase 'z'. For example, the return can be "ex.com/aazyus".

Then, when the user opens this shortened URL ("ex.com/aazyus") consisting of characters 'a'-'z', the browser opens the original URL ("veryyyyylongurl.com/example-long-extension").

Does that make sense?

**Candidate:** Sounds good. I understand the current set of features our application needs to support. In order to understand how much load this application would receive, are there any design constraints that we should look at in terms of scale?

## Step 2: Estimate

**Interviewer:** In terms of scalability, the only detail I will provide is that our service will need to support around 100 requests per second (RPS).

**Candidate:** Alright. In terms of expanding this RPS into design constraints for our problem, let's say we need to hold around 5 years' worth of URL conversions at one time.

**Interviewer:** How did you get five years?

**Candidate:** I believe five years is a good time frame to keep a link active. Although some estimates of one year or even three months may be valid, in order to produce results that don't risk user data loss, I believe five years is a good approximation.

Going from 100 RPS to a 5-year count, we need to be able to store ~16 B entries in our system.

$$\frac{100 \text{ requests}}{1 \text{ second}} * \frac{60 \text{ seconds}}{1 \text{ minute}} * \frac{60 \text{ minutes}}{1 \text{ hour}} * \frac{24 \text{ hours}}{1 \text{ day}} * \frac{365 \text{ days}}{1 \text{ year}} * 5 \text{ years} = 16B$$

Let's say we use the character set: [a-z, A-Z, 0-9]. That is a total of 62 characters. If we need to represent 16 B unique entries in our system with 62 characters, $\log_{62}(16\text{ B})$ will tell us how many characters we need in our system.

$$\log_{62} 16B = 5.69$$

We need at least 6 characters in our shortened URL to hold 5 years' worth of conversions.

**Interviewer:** Okay, that sounds fair to hold 5 years' worth of conversions for our users. Do you have a design decision behind why you chose 5 years?

**Candidate:** Although the usual lifetime of a URL conversion is short-lived on services such as TinyURL, I thought maintaining this information for a longer period of time would be useful. In addition, our service might be able to scrape old, shortened URLs for re-use if our service is maintained.

**Interviewer:** Okay. In terms of the estimated memory constraints, I believe we have a good idea of what we need to convert our long URLs into.

## Step 3: Design the service

**Candidate:** Great! From here, I'd like to move onto the workflow of our system, specifically the API.

**Interviewer:** Sure.

**Candidate:** Our feature set consists of two main functions, shortening a URL and expanding the shortened URL to the original URL. Thus, let's utilize GET and POST requests behind a single API endpoint called `/tinyurl`:

- A POST request to `/tinyurl` will convert a user's long URL and return a six-character URL.
- A GET request to `/tinyurl` will return the original URL from a six-character URL.

**Interviewer:** This API looks good. Doesn't look complicated at all and achieves what we need in terms of our feature set.

## Step 4: Articulate the data model

**Candidate:** Great! Now that we have our system's functionality done, I'd like to move towards our data model, specifically how we are going to store our data and what exactly we will store.

**Interviewer:** Sounds like a great directional move.

**Candidate:** For our database type. I'd like to select a SQL database because of its ACID properties. Atomic writes will help us in this situation since we may have multiple URL conversions happening at once. We can have one table representing all of our conversions that stores the time this conversion occurred, the long URL, and the short URL.

| MAIN | |
|---|---|
| uniqueID | INT |
| timestamp | DATE |
| shortURL | VARCHAR (6) |
| longURL | VARCHAR |

*MAIN Table Schema*

**Interviewer:** This looks like an appropriate table. I agree that one table should be enough to store the information we need for this problem. How do we plan on generating shortened URLs?

**Candidate:** To generate our shortened URL, there are several strategies we could use:

First, we could use a standard hashing algorithm that takes a long URL and converts it into a short one. Hashing algorithms, like MD5, can produce a 128 bit-string from any length string. This would force us to use 128 bits to represent our shortened URL.

Second, we could use a distributed global range monitor. Using a service such as Apache Zookeeper, we could designate ranges of ~1M IDs. From here each server would ping our Zookeeper to claim a range. Once each server runs out of unique IDs in its range, it goes back to the Zookeeper to attain another free range. Over time, different servers will create and write different ranges of IDs; however, all IDs will be stored in a single location.

For this problem, I believe using our Zookeeper range system would be highly beneficial because it allows us to represent our short URL in 36 bits rather than 128.

$$\frac{6 \text{ bits}}{1 \text{ character}} * \frac{6 \text{ characters}}{1 \text{ shortURL}} = \frac{36 \text{ bits}}{1 \text{ short URL}}$$

**Interviewer:** Alright, so this Zookeeper service we would use keeps track of ranges, such as 1 to 1,000,00; 1,000,001 to 2,000,00; 2,000,001 to 3,000,000; and so on. Each server then claims a range and gets 1M unique IDs to assign to the next 1,000,000 conversions in that server. This makes sense.

## Step 5: List the architectural components

**Candidate:** Perfect. Now, let's build a basic system architecture to handle the shortening and expanding workflows.

First, we can start with a simple server connected to a single database. This allows our system to shorten and expand a single URL. Although this is not a system that can support high load, it supports a straightforward workflow, nonetheless. Currently, we don't need our Zookeeper service since we only have one server. The Zookeeper service is useful for a distributed system.

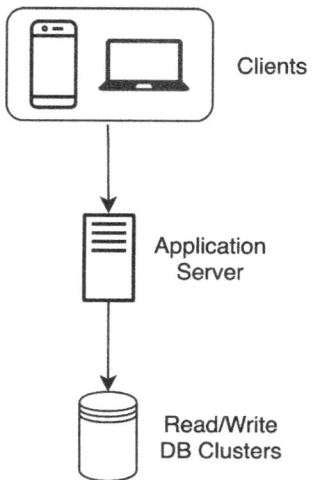

## Step 6: Scale

Now, let's scale our solution to handle more bandwidth. We can add a load balancer to handle a high request rate and select the freest server to hand the request off to. Our load balancer can use a simple round-robin algorithm to forward API requests. All of these servers then write to the same single database to keep track of our conversions.

Now that we have multiple servers, let's incorporate a Zookeeper to handle the issue of ranges.

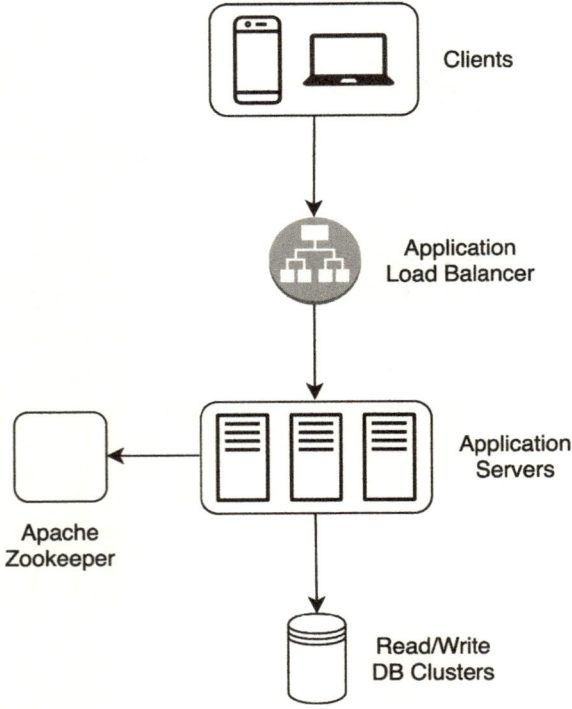

*The System Design Interview*

**Interviewer:** Alright. Our initial scaling makes sense. What do you see as primary concerns or issues to the newer system?

**Candidate:** Well, I can see that we read and write from the same database. This is an issue that can cause latency problems. We can remedy the problem with the main-replica database strategy.

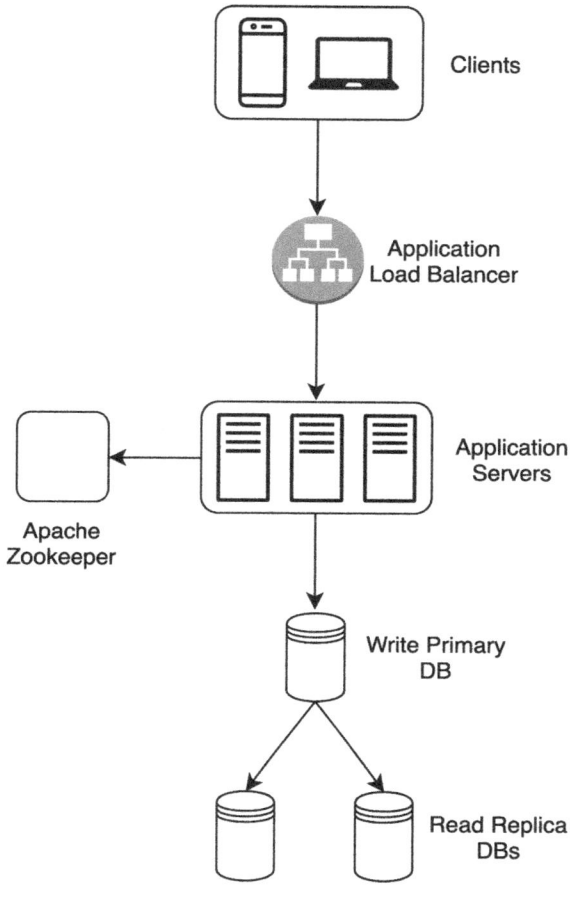

*The System Design Interview*

Likewise, we should separate our workflows for reads and writes. To do this, we can have a load balancer that accepts broad requests to our application and API routers that divide POST and GET requests to `/tinyurl` to the appropriate load balancers that then send the request to an available server.

The act of shortening a URL only occurs once while the expansions of that URL afterward may happen many times. Thus, we will have more reads than writes for our system. Our previous main-replica database strategy will help increase the availability of our system in this situation.

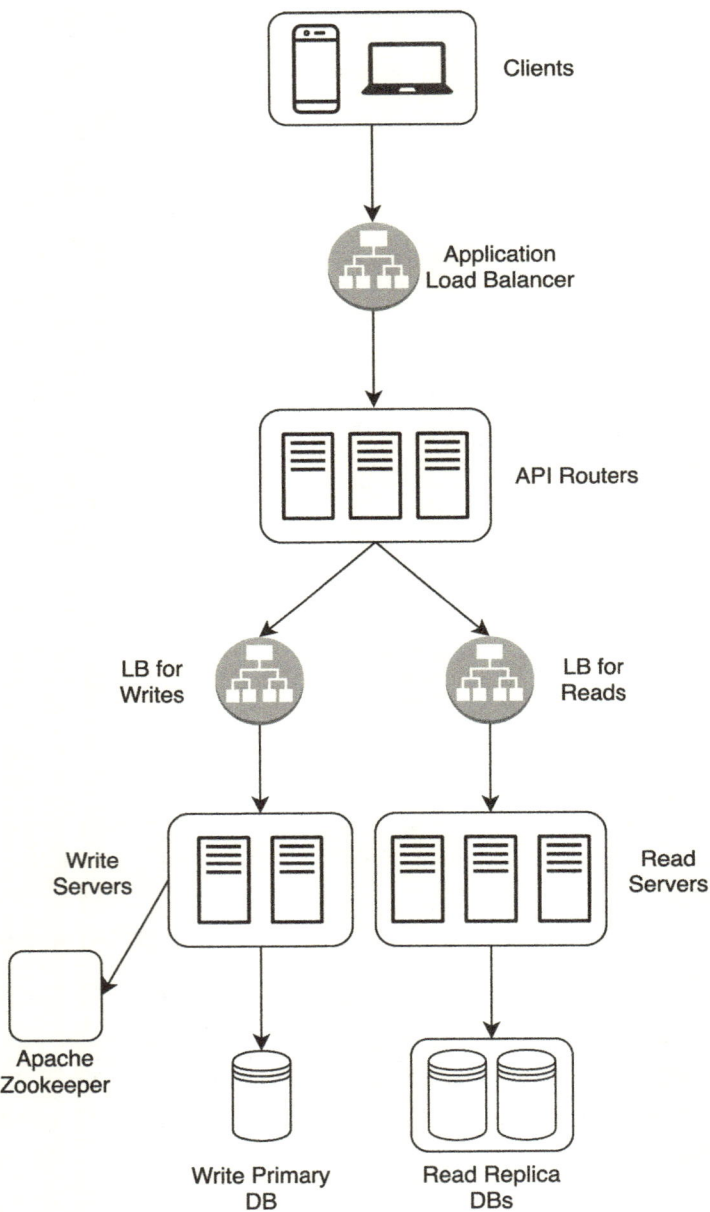

*The System Design Interview*

**Interviewer:** That looks good. We have solved many of the different scalability issues that I would look for. With our current solution, you said that our system is read-heavy than write-heavy, right? In that context, you mentioned that a separate read database system would alleviate our scalability problem. But I think there is an additional way we can optimize our system to achieve faster results. To give you a hint, we may not even need to hit our read replica.

**Candidate:** Hmm, give me a moment.

*The candidate takes a minute to think.*

I've already suggested the following to improve performance:

- Split reads from writes
- Create a main-replica relationship for faster reads
- Load balance the read/write workflows

I've got one more idea to make the system faster:

After creating a shortened URL, the user will likely access the new short URL after creating it. This leads me to believe that we are looking for something similar to temporal locality. A cache would make our system much faster on the reading side if we cached the mapping from short to long URLs. Perhaps we could use a Redis Cache to speed up reads that are close in time.

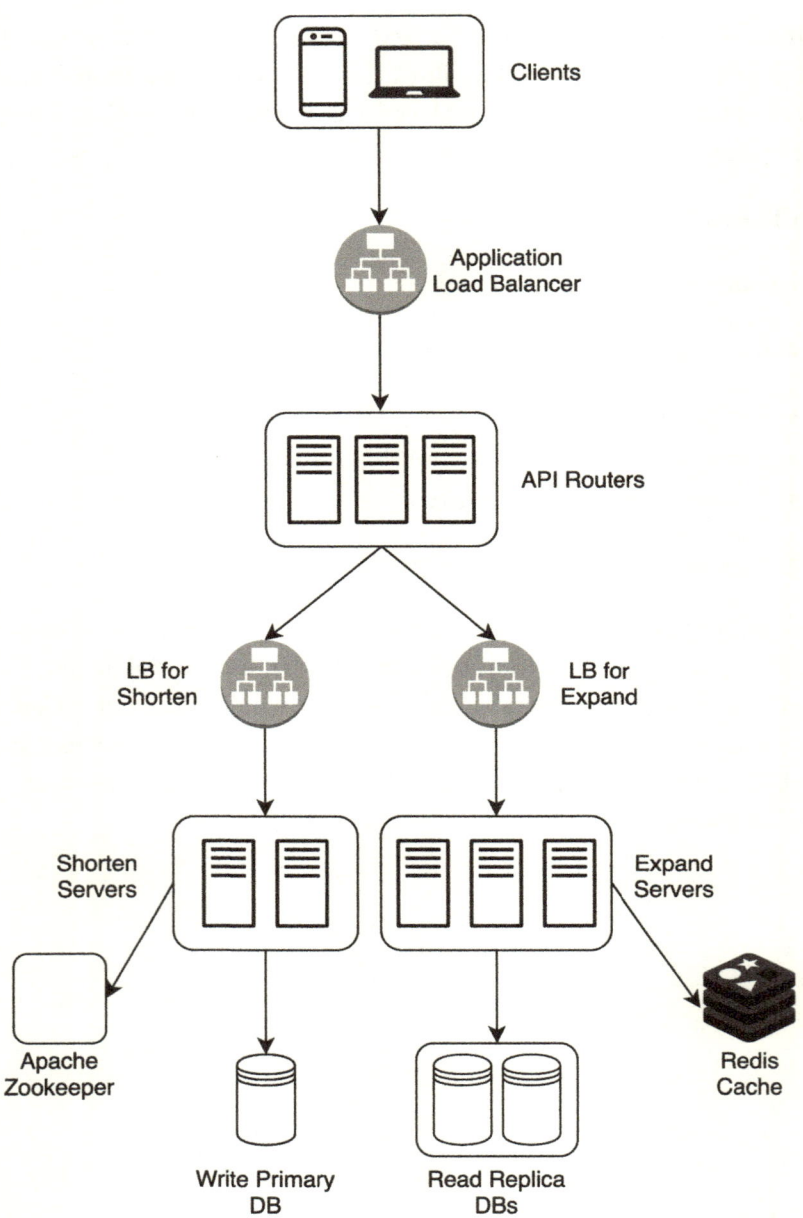

*The System Design Interview*

**Interviewer:** Exactly. After a user makes a shortened URL, accesses will likely occur in that local time frame because many users share the newly shortened URL immediately. That's why caching makes sense.

**Candidate**: Great. I believe our system handles scalability concerns well and maintains high availability. While the consistency between writes and reads may not be the best, it helps that the URL can't be used immediately so writes can be replicated. Other than what I described in this problem, do you have any other questions about my overall solution or thought process?

**Interviewer**: I have a question about the overall flow of events in your application. Can you explain to me how a single user's request is processed? Also, what happens when they try to access the URL after they create it?

**Candidate:** Sure, here's what happens when a user enters a long URL and requests a shortened version:

*Make a Short URL*

1. The request will hit our initial load balancer. The load balancer will then forward the request to the most available API router.
2. The request will be forwarded to the appropriate load balancer for the POST /tinyurl endpoint, which then forwards to an available server.
3. At the POST /tinyurl server, the server will check if it has a valid ID for the current request. If it doesn't, it'll go to the Zookeeper for a new range for the next 1M IDs.
4. The current ID will be converted from a number to a 6-character string that represents the shortened version of the long URL.
5. This conversion will then be written to the write database for later access during reads.
6. Once the database write is triggered, the server will return the short URL to the user.

*Request Short URL*

Next, when any browser attempts to use that shortened URL:

- Our initial load balancer will receive the short URL request.

- The initial load balancer will recognize it is a read operation and forward the request to the GET /tinyurl load balancer which will then forward to an appropriate read server.
- The read server will look up the short six-character URL in one of the read databases.
- The system will retrieve the longURL on that row that contains the original URL.
- The system will then redirect the user to the original URL.

**Interviewer:** Thank you.

# Design YouTube

**Things to Consider**
- Make sure to be thorough when explaining your design decisions

**Mistakes to Avoid**
- Don't think about the streaming service or unnecessary details during the problem
- Streaming mechanics in tech products create another problem that does not pertain to system design, but streaming is a good knowledge topic

**Interviewer:** Welcome! I've got a system design problem where we're building our version of YouTube, which we'll call VidWorld.

## Step 1: Process requirements

**Candidate:** Sounds perfect! What exactly does VidWorld entail?

**Interviewer:** VidWorld will have many of the basic YouTube features including uploading, streaming, and searching for videos.

**Candidate:** Okay. Besides watching user-generated content, does our system support liking & disliking videos? Can users comment on videos? Lastly, will VidWorld track metrics such as view count?

**Interviewer:** Got it. For the sake of time, let's focus on only implementing these six features:

1. Upload videos
2. Stream videos
3. Search for videos
4. Like and dislike
5. Add comments
6. See stats

**Candidate:** Okay. Just one quick clarifying question, when we implement comments, did you want me to support nested comments?

**Interviewer:** What do you mean by nested comments?

**Candidate:** Where users can reply to other comments.

**Interviewer:** To keep our comment system straightforward, let's say there are no comment replies, just single-level comments.

## Step 2: Estimate

**Candidate**: Okay. I think I understand the system requirements. I'd like to estimate the system load and storage required. How many users can we expect?

**Interviewer:** Let's say we have 1B users, 500M of which are active.

**Candidate:** Okay. I can take it from here. Since we have 500M active users, let's say that each user watches about 3 videos per day. That makes 1.5B views per day (500M * 3 views per day).

To understand how many videos are uploaded, we can estimate that for every 500 views, 1 video is uploaded to VidWorld. So, we have a 500:1 ratio in terms of views to uploads.

With 1.5B views per day, we get about 3M new videos daily (1.5B / 500 views per upload).

Lastly, I'd like to tackle our storage estimates. With 3M videos uploaded per day, I estimate each video is around 5 minutes in length. Each minute of a video takes around 50 MB, meaning each video is around a 250 MB storage cost. This gives us around 750 TB worth of content being uploaded to VidWorld each day.

**Interviewer:** How did you choose 50 MB per minute of video? Why not 100? Or 20?

**Candidate:** Most VidWorld content won't be uploaded in high video quality. By assuming an average of 720p, 30 frames per second, it's around ~60 MB per minute. So, taking 50 as a nice number was an approximation. Does that make sense?

**Interviewer:** Your figures seem reasonable to me. Though, why estimate how much content is being uploaded each day?

**Candidate:** Knowing how much content is being uploaded each day helps us estimate our data storage requirements. Some distributed file systems have capacity limits.

**Interviewer:** Good point. So now that we have our numbers together, where would you like to take this problem?

## Step 3: Design the service

**Candidate:** Now that we have our overall system requirements figured out, both the feature set and load capacity, I'd like to design the functionality behind our system. Specifically, an API outline would be great to understand how VidWorld will operate.

**Interviewer:** What are some concerns you might have when designing an API?

**Candidate:** I want to understand how VidWorld's desired functionality translates into technical specifications. Outlining how a system will work not only helps us design the system, but also provides a basic foundation for developing that system.

To start our discussion on API design, I want to break down our feature set and convert it into API endpoints.

For uploading content to VidWorld, we can set up an API endpoint called `/video` that takes in arguments such as the owner's `userID`, the `title` of the video, and the video content itself. This endpoint uploads the content with a POST request.

On the other hand, to view a video, a GET request to the `/video` endpoint returns the metadata for a specific video. The GET method to this route takes the current `userID`, `videoID`, and `second` offset into the video that the current client wants to retrieve.

**Interviewer**: Sorry, I'm a little confused. The `/video` endpoint can provide two different functionalities? How does that work?

**Candidate**: Yes, the different HTTP methods of the endpoint allow the endpoint to have different functionalities. When clients use a GET - request to the `/video` endpoint, they specify a different set of arguments and get metadata about a particular video on VidWorld. Similarly, if they use a POST request, they will provide information about a video they want to upload to VidWorld.

**Interviewer**: Sounds good. A more descriptive explanation the first time could have avoided this confusion.

**Candidate**: Good point. I agree.

If we stick with our API, we have two more features that we need to cover in terms of functionality.

For a user to retrieve content based on search queries, a simple GET endpoint called `/search` can ingest the `userID` and a search string called `searchStr` to indicate what the user is looking for. This endpoint can then return a list of video metadata that matches the user's search string.

Finally, when various search results are returned, thumbnails and fragments of the video's full data are displayed. To display all of the video's metadata, we create a separate API route `/metadata`. This API endpoint uses the GET method and takes the current `userID` as well as the `videoID`. The video's attributes, such as the number of views, likes, dislikes, and comments, are returned by this function so that clients can properly render the video page.

These endpoints should cover all the different functions of VidWorld.

To recap, we have the endpoints:

| Endpoint | Description |
| --- | --- |
| `GET /video` | Stream the video |
| `POST /video` | Upload user videos |
| `GET /search` | Search for videos given a query |

```
GET /metadata    Retrieve a video's metadata
```

**Interviewer:** Perfect. I think these endpoints cover our desired feature set and are named properly to describe exactly what they do.

## Step 4: Articulate the data model

**Candidate:** Let's move onto our data model to see how we store our data and metadata for VidWorld.

**Interviewer:** What are your concerns regarding a data model? What do you usually think about when you go about this process?

**Candidate:** It starts with data storage considerations, such as SQL vs NoSQL, or central server storage vs a distributed file system. For the most part, these are more or less straightforward; however, the tricky issues are around scalability with a data model.

Having a scalable data model is very important. It can alleviate pain points down the road when our user base increases and growth is important on our end.

**Interviewer:** That sounds reasonable. Let's tackle a general data model, first. Then, we can look into scalability issues. Just keep scalability in mind when designing an overall data model.

**Candidate:** Exactly. For this problem, we have two different issues to consider.

First, we need to store user's data such as username, creation date, and address. We also need to store video metadata like title, view count, likes, and date posted. For this task, I think it is simple enough to create a SQL database with multiple tables.

For user data, let's create a table called USERS that stores personal data such as username and password.

| USERS | |
|---|---|
| uniqueID | INT |
| firstName | VARCHAR(15) |

131

| | |
|---|---|
| lastName | VARCHAR(15) |
| username | VARCHAR(15) |
| password | VARCHAR(15) |
| DOB | DATE |
| creationTime | DATE |
| currentStatus | VARCHAR(15) |
| bio | VARCHAR(150) |

*USERS Table Schema*

We have our videos' metadata as well as comments left for data yet to store. Since comments can pile up extremely fast, separating comments from video metadata would be wise.

Let's create a table labeled as `VIDEOS` to store each video on a row with its appropriate metadata such as the view count, likes, and date posted.

| VIDEOS | |
|---|---|
| videoID | INT |
| title | VARCHAR (256) |
| descriptionStr | VARCHAR |
| datePosted | DATE |
| ownerID | STRING |
| contentPath | VARCHAR (1024) |
| likeCount | INT |
| dislikeCount | INT |
| viewCount | INT |

*VIDEOS Table Schema*

Lastly, let's create a `COMMENTS` table to store the videoID, comment text, as well as the time the comment was created.

| COMMENTS | |
|---|---|
| commentID | INT |
| userID | VARCHAR (256) |
| videoID | INT |
| commentText | DATE |
| postTime | STRING |

*COMMENTS Table Schema*

The second problem we face is the storage of raw video content. We estimate that 750 TB worth of data is uploaded every day. What design decisions would you advise when it comes to storing data of this magnitude?

**Interviewer**: I like how you've broken down the overall data model into sub-problems to effectively address them separately, since they don't have the same goal. In terms of storing video content, I would advise you to avoid single points of failure and try to minimize latency during user streaming.

**Candidate**: All right. To avoid single points of failure, I believe a good distributed data storage platform is Hadoop 2.0.

This technology allows us to have two main nodes that hold all the necessary metadata, and many different data nodes to store the actual video content. Having two main nodes avoids single points of failure in our system, and HDFS satisfies our storage constraint.

In our `VIDEOS` table, we store our video path. This path can correlate where the file is located throughout the HDFS cluster. We can easily connect our SQL database and our HDFS clusters to store our content on VidWorld at scale.

**Interviewer:** Okay. So now that our video content is stored on HDFS, how does our GET `/video` endpoint work?

**Candidate**: This GET endpoint is used to stream small portions of video to client devices. Clients will first request small segments of the video. This allows the client device to view the video immediately without waiting for the entire video to load first.

**Interviewer**: That's a good consideration. Shifting our product functionality by putting users first is a great strategy. Do you have any other talking points about the data model?

## Step 5: List the architectural components

**Candidate:** We have covered our data model well, so I'd like to move on to designing our system architecture and addressing scalability concerns.

To start, let's take a simple architecture approach. As we've discussed, we have an HDFS cluster as well as a single database with those three tables to keep track of. Let's use those two components and add an application server for VidWorld that interacts with both components. All client API requests will be supported through this single server.

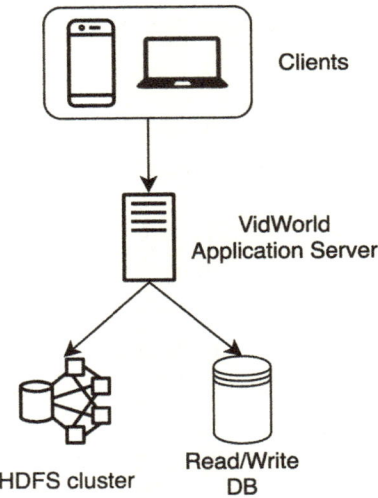

*The System Design Interview*

**Interviewer:** Alright. This looks like a good and basic start to our architecture design. Now, this obviously won't be able to meet any of our large-scale issues. How do you go about addressing these?

## Step 6: Scale

**Candidate:** For scalability, we have the following concerns:

- The large, global user base that wants to stream content
- 500:1 view-to-upload ratio, which means our system must be read optimized

To create a read-optimized system, let's split our read API code flow. A common strategy to split up and decentralize code flow is a microservice architecture.

Currently, our single server system is monolithic. To move towards a microservice architecture, let's create independent workflows so that services are clustered appropriately on their resource dependencies.

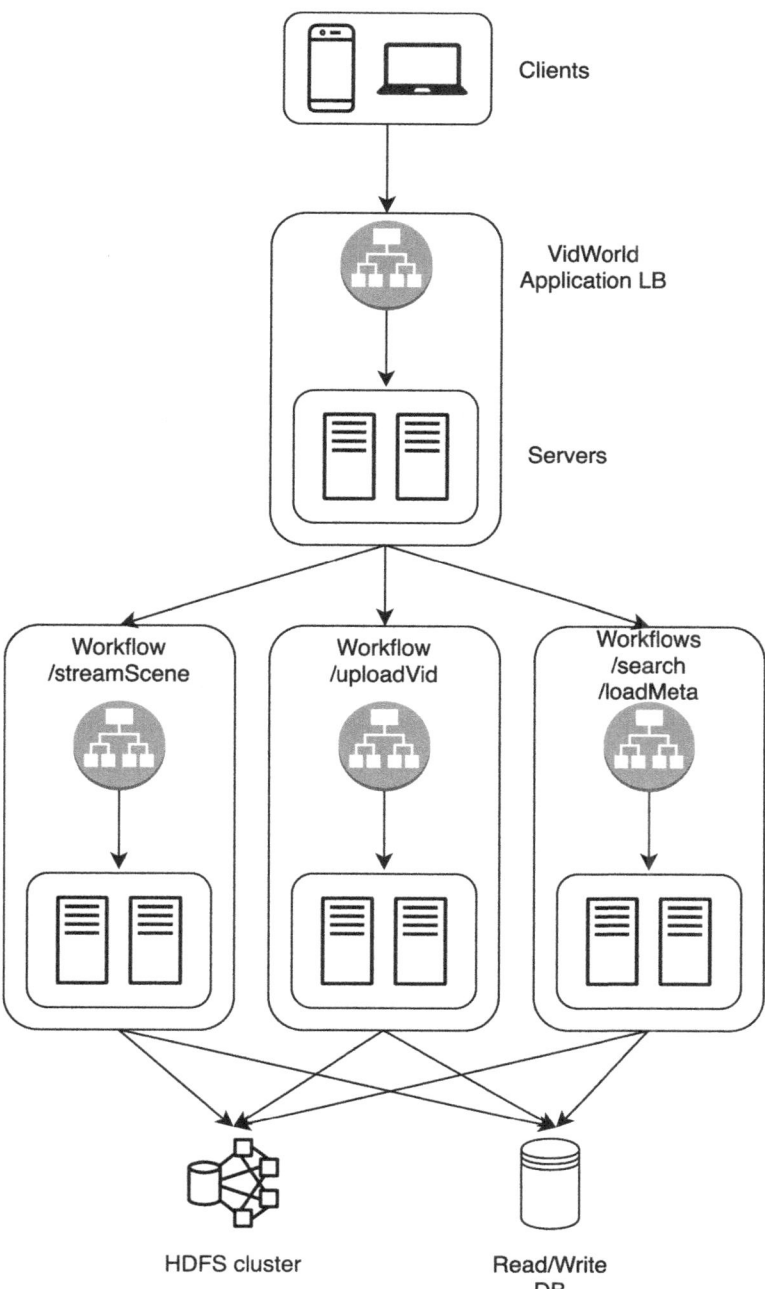

We now have an easier system to understand and construct.

With our current system, we provide a workflow to stream content to their client devices, which allows for our 500:1 view-to-upload ratio. But, even with our optimizations, we don't completely favor streaming content. We need another way to reduce latency.

There are two ways to do so.

The first solution is to create read replica databases to make searching content and loading metadata faster.

Although the consistency between uploading content and searching for it immediately afterwards is not the best, once the content is replicated to the Read Replica servers, it is much faster to find.

We also serve content to users all over the world. This means that querying our HDFS cluster for streaming content may not be the fastest solution. The second solution is to use a content delivery network to speed up this process.

CDNs can cache various responses in servers that are close to users, which improves latency. Now users don't have to fetch content all the way from our HDFS cluster; instead, local CDN servers store that data, allowing VidWorld to respond and load faster.

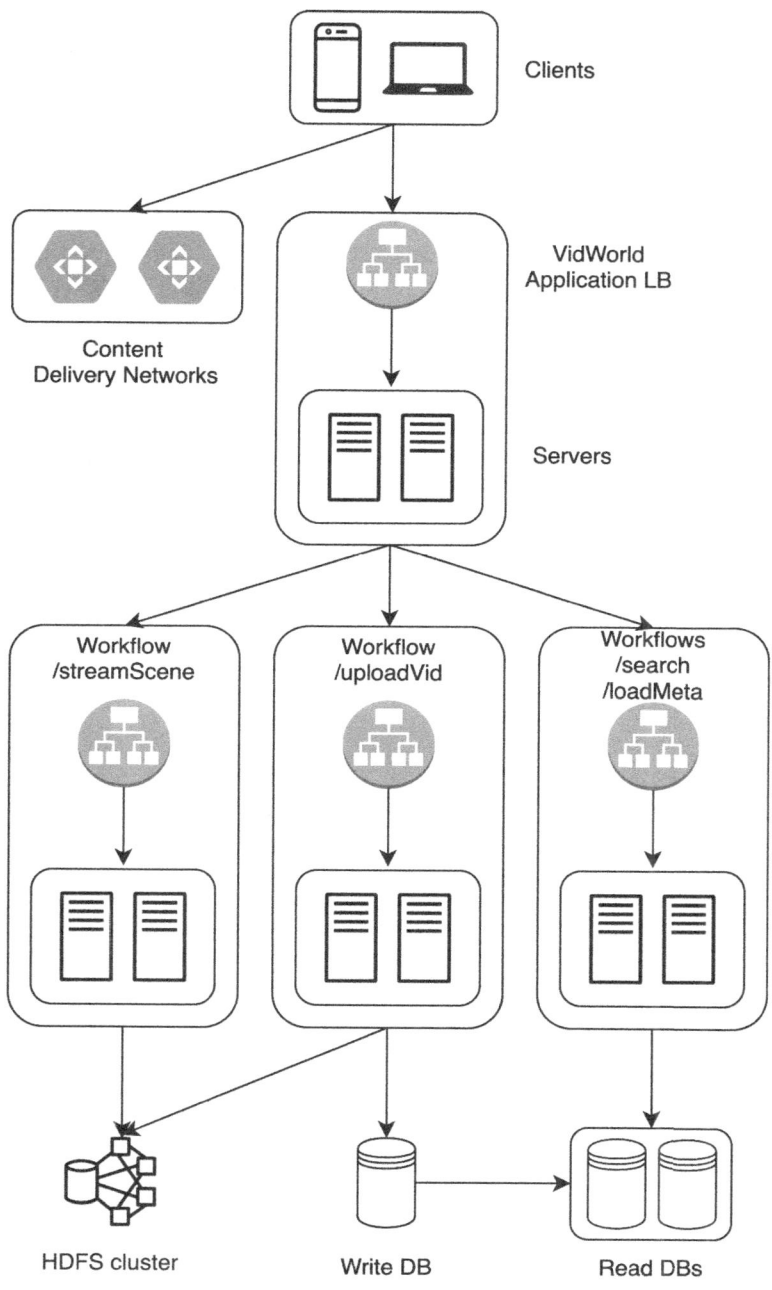

*The System Design Interview*

**Interviewer:** Great! That looks like a system that can handle lots of data.

**Candidate:** That's great to hear. There are other database optimizations we can do like sharding with hashing. Would you like me to implement that or other suggestions?

**Interviewer:** I feel what we have now is great. The main emphasis of this exercise was to see a distributed file storage system and a CDN. It is great that you know about sharding and other database techniques, but for now, this system is good.

**Candidate**: Perfect! Do you have any other questions for me regarding my thought process or anything related to system design?

**Interviewer**: Not at the moment. You've done a good job demonstrating your knowledge of system design.

**Candidate:** Thanks! I enjoyed designing VidWorld.

# Design WhatsApp

**Things to Consider**
- Consider the security of user messages on the platform
- Ensure you address scale to the right degree

**Mistakes to Avoid**
- Ensure you address scale to the right degree

**Interviewer:** Thanks for coming today! To start off our interview, I want to take a look at a system design problem.

**Candidate:** Perfect! What are we designing?

**Interviewer:** In this problem, we're going to model our system around an online chat application such as WhatsApp or GroupMe. We want to be able to support one-to-one messages and group messages.

## Step 1: Process requirements

**Candidate:** Got it. Can users send content like photos or videos? Should we also support sent, delivered, and read notifications?

**Interviewer:** Yes. Let's say we support these features. Sending photos and videos is allowed. We also notify users that their message has been sent, delivered, or read. To address this issue, our system only supports mobile clients and does not need to store messages on the server. Clients can handle storing messages locally.

**Candidate:** Oh, that's great! That makes our problem a little less complex. Does our solution support users' status like active or idle? How about a notification that they are typing?

**Interviewer:** Great ideas. I didn't think of that. If we have time at the end, we should add those features. Does that sound good?

## Step 2: Estimate

**Candidate**: Sounds perfect! To understand how much demand there will be for our system, do you have any numbers I could work with in terms of user base?

**Interviewer:** I don't have a lot of details to provide you; however, let's say our platform supports roughly 750M users, 500M of which message at least once a day.

**Candidate:** With 500M active users daily that means 500M messages per day. Now let's convert that number of messages per second:

$$\frac{500M \text{ active users}}{24 \text{ hours}} * \frac{1 \text{ hour}}{60 \text{ minutes}} * \frac{1 \text{ minute}}{60 \text{ seconds}} = \frac{5{,}800 \text{ messages}}{\text{second}}$$

This figure helps us understand how many requests our server will receive around the clock.

**Interviewer:** This is a good approximation of the real-time demand our system could have. How do you plan to use this number in designing our system?

**Candidate:** This figure can help us scale our system appropriately to ensure latency isn't an issue. With this estimate, I'd like to move toward designing the functionality of our system.

**Interviewer:** Perfect.

## Step 3: Design the service

**Candidate:** Generally, chat applications don't use HTTPS and standard API calls to bridge client-server communication. Instead, web sockets are a common tactic that allows live connections between clients and application servers.

I envision a system where clients use this socket connection to send message packets to servers in a standardized format that specifies the recipientID and message content.

**Interviewer:** What type of connection would you use?

**Candidate:** TCP.

**Interviewer:** Why is that?

**Candidate**: TCP requires the receiver to acknowledge receipt of data with a 3-way handshake known by the abbreviations SYN, ACK, and SYN-ACK.

**Interviewer:** Continue.

**Candidate**: In most cases, clients will send text over these connections; however, since photos, videos, and other multimedia content are also supported, we need a way to store the content on our platform. We can address this issue with 2 different API endpoints: one to upload the content to our system and another to retrieve the media on the receiving end.

To send multimedia content, let's open an endpoint called `/content` that takes the file object and an authentication token through a POST request. This allows users to upload their content to our system that can be sent to other users. This endpoint returns a unique identifier for that file that is sent to the recipients of the message. These recipients will use this identifier to get the file from our servers.

To receive media, the same `/content` endpoint can be used but with a GET request. This GET method of the `/content` endpoint takes in the uniqueID of the content and an authentication key. This endpoint returns the file to the recipient's client.

This covers the basics for sending messages and files through our platform.

**Interviewer**: So you're saying that clients send text messages over web sockets and files over API requests via HTTPS? How does the recipient know to make an API request to our server with the correct file identifier?

**Candidate**: When a file is sent through our system, the clients make the API request to upload to our servers. Once the API returns the identifier for that file, the client sends that identifier to the recipient via the websocket.

Once the receiver's device receives that identifier, it will make the appropriate API request with that identifier to retrieve the desired file.

**Interviewer**: I see. That flow makes sense. So you plan to use the web socket connection to send the file identifier. How are you going to mask the identifier in a text message so that the recipient knows not to play back the actual text of that message, but to make the appropriate API call with the identifier?

**Candidate**: We can create a standard, platform-wide packet header that delineates that certain messages should not be rendered. Instead, they should be used as internal components of the system.

**Interviewer**: A header that signals that a particular message should not be rendered?

**Candidate**: Exactly. That should achieve the functionality we want. In fact, we can use the same header strategy to send status updates to any message. This allow us to achieve our "sent", "delivered", and "read" status updates via messages that use the same header but contain different flags.

**Interviewer**: Uh-huh. We can call different functions while using the same API call.

## Step 4: Articulate the data model

**Candidate:** You got it. This header strategy allows the application to have an internal communication system. Since we have communication methods and functionality designed, I'd like to move forward with creating a data model that can support our current intention.

**Interviewer:** Alright. What do you need to achieve with this data model? Besides functionality, what are we missing in order to reach a full system?

**Candidate:** Well, our system primarily relies on web sockets. This means that we need to have an active client connection to deliver messages. If recipients are not connected to our system, our platform is responsible for storing these messages to later send to the user when they connect.

To achieve this, we need some sort of data store such as SQL or NoSQL.

Initially, I'm thinking of a SQL database that has rows of messages that are to be sent to users. However, HBase better fits our needs. It's a NoSQL database known for fast random reads and writes.

HBase is a distributed database built upon BigTable and HDFS, so we have partition tolerance and spatial locality. HBase's features allow our servers to immediately find pending messages for users when they connect to one of our servers.

In our HBase database, let's create a PENDING table where we store the recipientID, internal headers, and the message content. As we discussed, since status update indications are also plain messages that use different header types, we can also send the status updates of message delivery and read receipts through this table.

| PENDING | |
|---|---|
| uniqueID | INT |
| creationTime | DATE |
| senderID | INT |
| recipientID | INT |
| msgHeader | VARCHAR |
| msgContent | VARCHAR |

*PENDING Table Schema*

Another pain point of our system is the effect of using web sockets. Since web sockets consume a server's port, we need many ports, to be available to users, across different servers. This means we need to allocate multiple servers to scale our system horizontally. However, when a user sends a message to a user connected to a different server, our system needs to have a stateful map of users and their connection status. This allows our system to map that message to the correct server the other user is connected to.

To further explain this, let's say we have user A and user B. User A is connected to server 1, while user B is connected to server 2. When user A sends a message to user B, server 1 receives this message. However, server 1 is not connected to user B. So, how can server 1 send the message to user B? It needs to know what server user B is connected to if any. That's why we need an internal, stateful mapping of users to their connection status.

One solution is a SQL database with a USERS table. This table can simply hold the `userID` to `serverID` relationship. If a user is not connected to our system, the `serverID` can be set to an impossible value such as -1. This will send a message to our PENDING database, where it will wait until the recipient is connected to our platform again.

| USERS | |
|---|---|
| uniqueID | INT |
| userID | INT |
| serverID | INT |

*USERS Table Schema*

**Interviewer:** I can see this working for 1:1 chats. What about group chats? How do we deal with this issue?

**Candidate:** We need to store group associations separately. For example, we can have an entry for each user in a group that holds a `groupID` to `userID` relationship.

| GROUPS | |
|---|---|
| uniqueID | INT |
| groupID | INT |
| userID | INT |

*GROUPS Table Schema*

When a user in a group chat sends a message:

- We iterate through the entries on the GROUPS table that match the specified `groupID`
- Find the appropriate `userIDs` in this group

- Look up the servers connected to each of these users in our USERS table.
- Send the message to each user through the appropriate server, found during our USERS table lookup.

**Interviewer:** Okay, but I see a flaw. If groups are too large, iterating through all of these users and performing constant lookups may severely slow down our system. How can we alleviate this issue?

**Candidate:** I see a quick fix. We can limit the number of members in our group chats to around ~50 users for now. After launching the system, we may toggle this threshold by analyzing performance on different group chat sizes.

**Interviewer:** Toggling this lever is a great strategy to understand our system's performance constraints and adapting to them. I like this approach.

## Step 5: List the architectural components

**Candidate:** Thanks! Now that we have the data model as well as all our functionality constraints out of the way, let's move forward to our platform's architecture.

I am planning on initially starting with a baseline system and scaling it appropriately to meet our capacity estimations.

Let's start with an HBase database to keep our:

- Pending messages
- Group chat tracking database

Then let's have an HDFS to store content sent via our API endpoints.

We don't need our user-to-server tracking database since all sessions are through a single server.

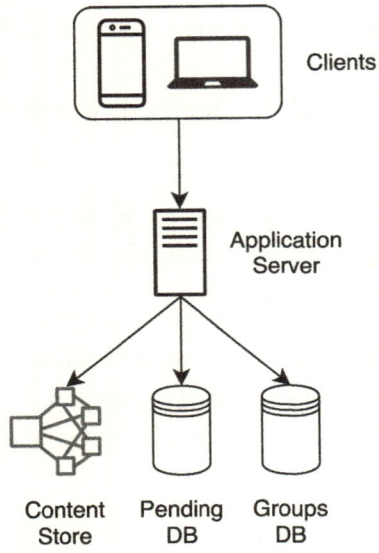

## Step 6: Scale

**Candidate:** From here, we horizontally scale to increase the number of servers. This will allow our platform to maintain more web socket connections, serving more users concurrently. In order to add more servers in this horizontal scaling, we should front them with a load balancer to even demand across our servers. Since we have more than one server at this point, users can converse between servers, meaning we need our USERS database table at this point.

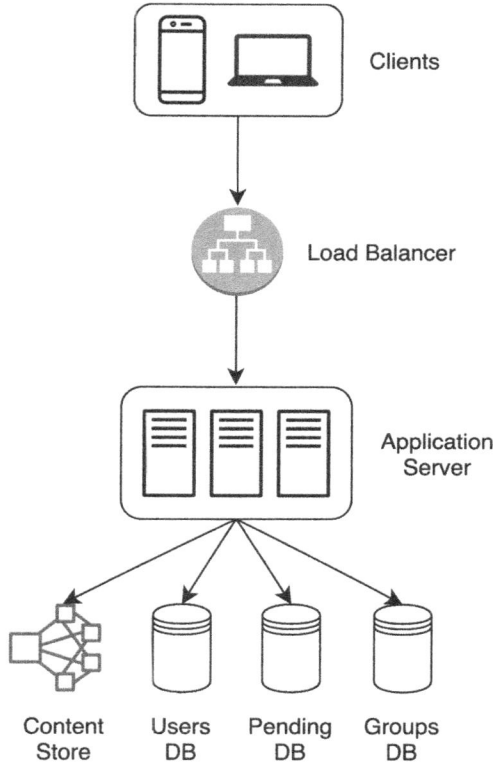

*The System Design Interview*

With this current design, our platform should meet our capacity requirements and also be performant in handling requests.

**Interviewer:** This looks like a good solution. It may be performant with our current requirements; however, given messaging demands are at peak levels in the morning, how can we further optimize our system to perform better at peak-time as well?

**Candidate:** To further increase our system's performance, we can shard our pending messages NoSQL database into four subsystems. This will decrease latency.

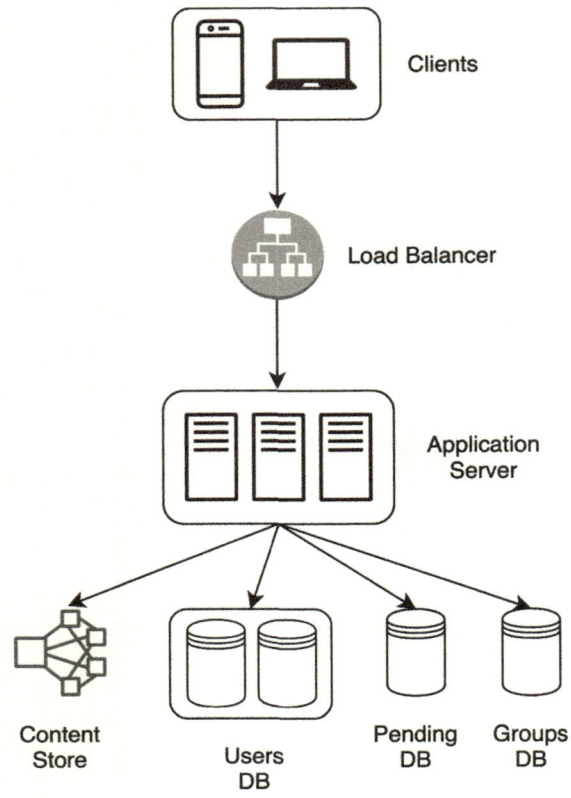

*The System Design Interview*

**Interviewer:** Although what you have presented makes our system more performant, I don't believe this is the solution I am looking for. There is another route I am looking for.

**Candidate:** Okay. Let me think for a little bit to look for areas our system may be able to improve.

What I can see as a vulnerability for our system are our USERS and GROUPS databases. SQL allows for concurrent reads to tables but does not allow for simultaneous reads and writes on the same table since it uses *transactions* and *locking mechanisms* to provide consistent data.

For example, if we were to update a user's active connection status from server A to server B, the table would need to be locked to update this request. This creates a bottleneck by preventing concurrent reads to the same table.

To alleviate the bottleneck, we can create read replicas for faster read access.

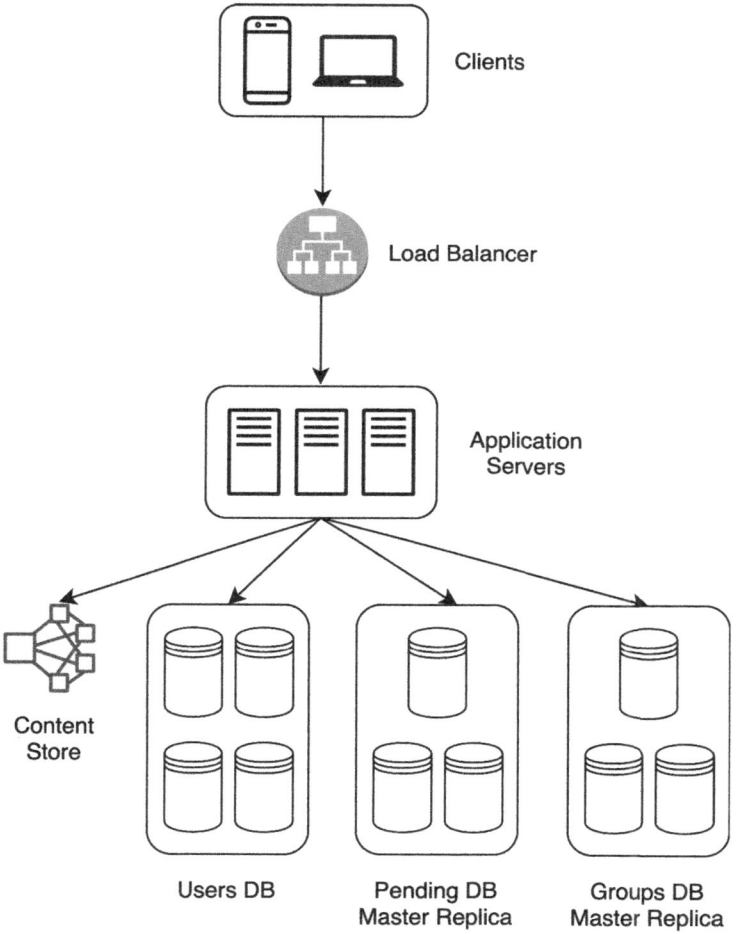

*The System Design Interview*

This read replica will increase our availability and overall throughput. Also, I don't think we need to worry about consistency as much for these tables because:

- Group chats don't often change in size.

- Pending requests will only be looked at once and delivered at mass. Deletion will occur after and re-reads won't happen to these entries.

**Interviewer:** Perfect! Now we have a system that minimizes bottlenecks.

Although some in the industry claim replicas reduce consistency, the benefit of increased availability and throughput outweigh those costs. Your reasoning for why these tables are viable for read replicas is sound.

Can we extend this same read replica strategy to the USERS database?

**Candidate:** We can, in theory, extend this to the USERS database. Despite this, I would advise against it to maintain a high level of consistency here. Because replication can cause latency issues, I would not advise having stale data when redirecting requests to a potentially misaligned server. Taking the hit in terms of availability to maintain high consistency in an area where we have time-sensitive data is important.

**Interviewer:** Good point. I agree! That table keeps time-sensitive data where we want to maintain consistency.

**Candidate:** Great! Do you have any other questions regarding the system or my thought process throughout the duration of this interview?

**Interviewer:** No. This looks like a great system. Well done.

# Design Unique ID Generator

*For a different approach, research Twitter Snowflake's design and implementation for a different implementation of this problem.*

**Things to Consider**
- How can a distributed system handle a single incremental value?
- Consider solutions to handing out unique identifiers with several machines?

**Mistakes to Avoid**
- Don't forget to consider solutions to handing out unique identifiers with several machines

**Interviewer:** Welcome! I hope you're doing well. Today, I wanted to go over a unique system design problem.

## Step 1: Process requirements

**Candidate:** Good afternoon! That sounds great. What is our system's purpose?

**Interviewer:** When people join large-scale platforms such as Facebook, Gmail, Twitter, or Instagram, they need an internal identifier, correct?

**Candidate:** Yes, that's how companies identify users. Isn't it called a global unique identifier (GUID) or a universal unique identifier (UUID), right?

**Interviewer:** Exactly. Our system's purpose is to generate these globally unique identifiers so they can assign them to users when they join the platform. The official outline of the problem is:

*Design a system that can generate a unique identifier for users when they join a platform such as Facebook. This platform will support around 1B users in its lifespan. Additionally, you can expect these requests for unique identifiers to occur concurrently. Meaning, your system should support retrieving user identifiers for multiple requests at the same time.*

As a side note, generating monotonically increasing user IDs is not important to us. Make sure to note this as you design your solution.

**Candidate:** Ok, this is interesting. The concurrency requirement makes this problem more complicated than implementing a single server with a local variable.

**Interviewer:** Precisely.

## Step 2: Estimate

**Candidate:** How many requests per second should we expect?

**Interviewer:** Can you estimate that for me?

**Candidate:** Sure. We need a system can handle 1B users.

The first thing I'm thinking about is how many bits we need to express 1B; this tells us how many bits our user IDs need to be:

$$\log_2 1{,}000{,}000{,}000 = 29.897$$

For 1B users, we would need 30 bits. To make it easier, let's use a standard 32-bit integer to handle this case. That means our system can potentially hold 4.2B, or $2^{32}$, users.

**Interviewer:** Let's say our 1B users will join this platform over a span of 5 to 8 years. However, you should note that growth trends with these applications will follow an S-curve. We don't want to re-engineer this system with increased growth rates.

**Candidate:** That's understandable. With something as pivotal as generating user IDs, we don't want this system to curb the growth of any application.

As you said our 1B users will join this platform over the next 5 to 8 years. Let's take the most aggressive situation and engineer off of that: 5 years.

$$\frac{1B \text{ users}}{5 \text{ years}} * \frac{1 \text{ year}}{365 \text{ days}} * \frac{1 \text{ day}}{24 \text{ hours}} * \frac{1 \text{ hour}}{60 \text{ minutes}} = \frac{7 \text{ requests}}{1 \text{ second}}$$

That gives us around 7 requests per second on average. Do you disagree with this estimate?

**Interviewer:** No. Looks good to me. Proceed.

## Step 3: Design the service

**Candidate:** I'd like to design our service's general functionality, specifically an API.

Our service should fit into a microservice architecture. That means other services will ping our service for a new UUID. An API for this functionality should allow our component to fit right in.

Since our application only has one real feature, let's open an endpoint `/uuid` to abstractly handle this responsibility with a GET request.

This is the only endpoint this system will need. I'd like to move on to designing the specific functionality of this endpoint to generate those user IDs.

**Interviewer:** How are you looking at designing this system? What is the overall concept behind this design?

**Candidate:** I'd like to take a closer look into our 32-bit value.

I know Unix timestamps are also 32 bits. Given a request, we can convert the current time into a Unix timestamp, which is granular to the second. Since we have multiple requests per second, we can allocate multiple servers to handle those concurrent requests. At an expected seven requests per second, let's allocate 16 servers.

I chose 16 servers as an easy measure to have excess compute power above our current expected RPS. Thus, during peak times, we can manage increased loads without provisioning additional compute power.

Likewise, we can use bit manipulation techniques to create a pre-set number of servers. What I mean by this is that we can use four bits to identify servers: four bits can take on 16 values. Choosing one less bit would decrease our available servers to eight, which might falter during peak usage.

We can append these 4 bits to the front of our 32-bit timestamp. We now have a 36-bit value.

$\underbrace{0100}_{\text{Server ID}}\ \underbrace{11010011101001010011010010101010}_{\text{User ID}}$

This should be able to handle our design constraint of not only supporting at least 1B users but also handling multiple requests per second.

**Interviewer:** I like your approach in converting a timestamp into a 32-bit value and further solving with multiple servers. Will we have a round-robin load balancer to spread out incoming requests?

**Candidate:** Yes, we will delegate the requests across our 16 servers. To further prevent this, we can queue requests at peak hours to force each server to one unique ID per second.

**Interviewer:** Interesting approach, but I don't think it will work. Here's why:

- You created multiple servers to respond to concurrent requests, based on the estimation, to avoid duplicate identifiers.
- You queued excess requests to throttle each server to one request per second, to avoid duplicate identifiers.
- Lastly, you took the worst-case scenario to engineer a system that would provide the best performance.

But the weak point of this system, which will almost guarantee failure, is the reliance on time. Have you heard of NTP?

**Candidate:** Yes. I have heard of the phrase before. It stands for Network Time Protocol, correct? It keeps clocks on multiple servers aligned since clocks can naturally drift.

**Interviewer:** Exactly. Let's say one of our servers has a clock that drifts too far in the future. While the system is out in production, that server's clock is ~3 seconds ahead.

The NTP clock recognizes this issue and recalibrates its clock. Now we are at an accurate time. But the issue is that we have already assigned 3 identifiers in the "future". As our server begins to process requests, it re-assigns those timestamps as UUIDs to different users. See the problem?

At this point, we have 3 pairs of users who have the same identifier.

**Candidate:** Ohhh. This is a major issue. As you mentioned this all comes back to relying on a clock to assign identifiers.

**Interviewer:** Yes.

Not to mention, during dead periods, where we don't get 1 request per second for each of our servers, we are wasting away identifiers. This creates gaps in our global set of user IDs.

This is another pain point you would have to address and using a clock cannot solve this issue.

**Candidate:** I understand. I don't think this clock approach can overcome these issues you mentioned.

Instead, I'd like to take a different strategy. A solution to this problem would also have to overcome the issue of wasted identifiers and concurrency.

**Interviewer:** Take your time to think of a solution that can work.

**Candidate:** Hmm...

I believe using ranges in a central server could work. Let's say we have batches of ranges from 1 to 2B. For example, ranges such as 1 - 1,000,000, 1,000,001 - 2,000,000, and so on.

We can orchestrate these ranges such that an application server can claim a range when it does not have one or runs out of identifiers in the range it previously owned. Once it has a range, the server can keep a local variable to understand its position within the range as it assigns new user IDs.

These servers can claim ranges from a central microservice that orchestrates the assignment of ranges.

**Interviewer:** Interesting. We have one central service that understands all of the available ranges and application servers that claim them from this service. Once an application server claims a range, how does it operate?

**Candidate:** These application servers start a local variable at the beginning of that range and increment or assign these user IDs until it reaches the max of its assigned range.

For example, let's say server A claims the range 3,000,001 - 4,000,000. The first request after this range claim would receive the user ID 3,000,001. Then the server would increment its current place within the range and return 3,000,002 to the next user. This goes on until the server gives up user ID 4,000,000. At that point, the application server would go to the central server for the next available range and continue the same pattern.

The interesting note here is that when multiple servers concurrently respond to client requests, the user IDs given out will not be monotonically increasing globally. They will only be monotonically increasing with respect to each server, individually. Since monotonically increasing userIDs are not a requirement of this system, this solution is viable.

**Interviewer:** Okay this makes sense. Have you ensured this does not run into the same issues your previous solution had?

**Candidate:** Let's run through those situations to ensure it does not.

To the issue of multiple users receiving the same user ID. Each application server can respond to multiple requests concurrently by locking around a global value for the next identifier to allocate. Each of the N requests in the system will then attempt to retrieve this value, but the value will be handed out to each request individually, avoiding duplicate identifiers.

With wasting valuable identifiers, our service only hands out the next possible identifier when it is requested. That means this system avoids throwing away those valuable values.

By running through those two situations, it looks like our solution avoids the gaps in the previous strategy I mentioned.

**Interviewer:** Okay. Where do you want to head from here now that you have a general idea of how the system will perform?

## Step 4 & 5: Articulate the data model & List the architectural components

**Candidate:** With our functionality solidified, I'd like to dive into the details of a data model. The only data-related issue we have is to store ranges that we can hand out to application servers.

We can use a fancy solution such as Apache Zookeeper. However, I believe a single server that writes to a file that specifies the availability of range can do our job. So, we can have a single `rangeKeeper` microservice that knows the taken and available ranges. It can understand this by writing out to a file the status of these ranges.

## Step 6: Scale

**Interviewer:** I like the simplicity of your approach, but is this not a single point of failure?

**Candidate:** Yes. It is a single point of failure that we can remedy with a failover server. This other server can hand out ranges in the situation where the primary `rangeKeeper` server fails. The file to keep track of these ranges can be shared between both servers.

**Interviewer:** Makes sense.

**Candidate:** To recap what we have discussed; we have a cluster of application servers that respond to client requests for Universal User IDs and a microservice to hand out these ranges.

To address our scale constraint, let's have a cluster of 4 servers that respond to client requests.

**Interviewer:** Great. This seems like a fair approach. But how do clients reach these individual servers?

**Candidate:** For that, we can front our system with a load balancer that can take care of evenly routing traffic across our cluster. Does this make sense?

**Interviewer:** Perfect. Does our system address our scale requirements?

**Candidate:** I believe it does. With our set of 4 servers, we can easily handle the approximate 7 requests per second threshold.

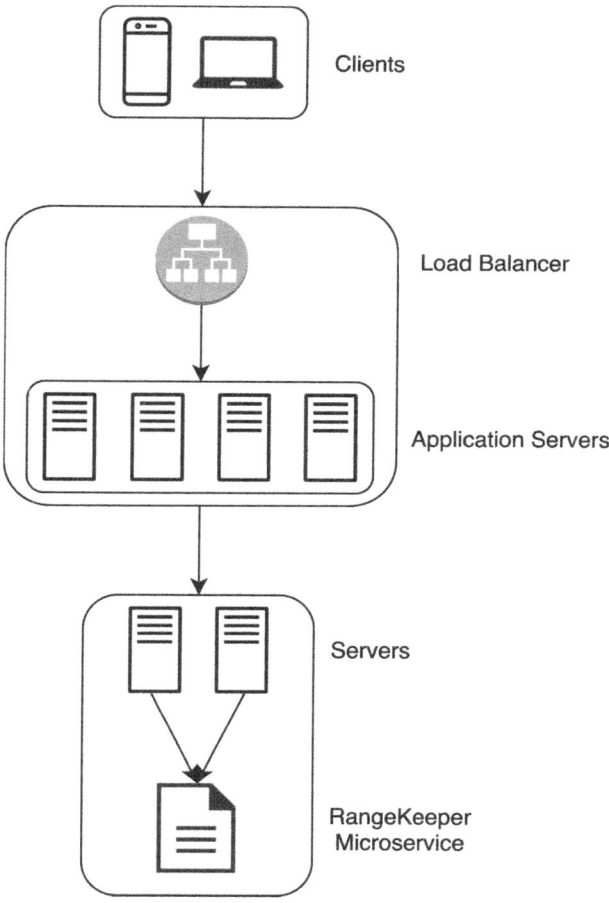

*The System Design Interview*

On the other hand, our microservice will not be under great stress since it is pinged by each server for every million new users.

**Interviewer:** Ok. This all makes sense, and it performs better than the clock strategy we discussed earlier.

Since we now have a working solution, why didn't you choose to use a single database that can generate monotonically increasing user IDs?

**Candidate:** Well since monotonically increasing user IDs was not of great importance to us, it eliminated that strategy's greatest strength. In addition, our system would be severely bottlenecked to the time that a single database would need to write an entry.

An approach that uses this database strategy would also lead to a single point of failure. To address this, we could have replicated this data into a read-only database to recover, given a failure event. However, we would have to give up consistency in this replication between databases that would also lead to errors in our identifier generation.

**Interviewer:** I didn't even think of that. That's a good explanation. Your solution robustly handles high demand. It's also consistent, available, and reliable. Well done.

**Candidate:** Thanks! Do you have any questions regarding my solution or thought process throughout this interview?

**Interviewer:** I don't believe so. You did a great job recovering from your first solution. Thanks for coming in.

# Design Auto-Suggest

**Things to Consider**
- Always provide reasoning for your assumptions
- Draw high-level designs to support your explanations

**Mistakes to Avoid**
- Failure to address trade-offs
- Failure to acknowledge the interviewer's concerns

**Interviewer:** Good Morning! We're going to solve a system design problem around auto-suggesting on a mobile phone.

For example. when you type in a search on Google, it predicts what you intend to search for. That's what we're going to design together today. Sound good to you?

## Step 1: Process requirements

**Candidate:** Sounds great! If I understand it correctly, as you type, you'll get a real-time prediction for the search, character by character, right?

**Interviewer:** Yes, exactly. So as the user types, the system updates for each character and predicts a new set of search queries that the user may intend to search.

**Candidate:** All right. Besides what we've discussed, are there any other details that I should understand before I get into the problem?

**Interviewer:** No. What we've discussed so far should cover the basics.

## Step 2: Estimate

**Candidate:** Great. With our current problem scope, I'd like to understand the capacity needed for our solution.

**Interviewer:** The only detail I'm allowed to tell you is that our system will take roughly 5 requests per second. With this, you may decide to extrapolate or continue to design an appropriate system.

**Candidate:** I think extrapolating further to understand how many requests we receive per day would be a good route. With around 5 requests per second, we're looking at roughly 430K requests daily.

$$\frac{5 \text{ requests}}{1 \text{ second}} * \frac{60 \text{ seconds}}{1 \text{ minute}} * \frac{60 \text{ minutes}}{1 \text{ hour}} * \frac{24 \text{ hours}}{1 \text{ day}} = \frac{432 \text{ K requests}}{1 \text{ day}}$$

With this number in mind, we understand our demand and can proceed to take a look at a broad overview of how we should design our system.

## Step 3: Design the service

**Interviewer:** What do you mean by a broad overview? What do you plan to design first for our final system?

**Candidate:** I'd design our API first. In my experience, knowing the general workflow of a system helps tremendously in designing the system architecture.

**Interviewer:** Got it. Go ahead and design the API.

**Candidate:** This problem area is not that complex because there is only one workflow. Clients can ping a server with the currently entered search phrase and expect a response with a list of predicted search queries from our system.

For this communication stream, we can open a single GET endpoint labeled `/suggestions`.

Beyond this endpoint, I don't see the need to support other API endpoints. We can abstract the entire workflow behind this API endpoint and begin to understand how we will design the functionality behind such an abstraction.

**Interviewer:** Hmm. Is there any point in designing an API if there's only one supported endpoint?

**Candidate:** I think designing the API helps us understand the overall technical feature set. It gives us a direction as well as definitive milestones to achieve in terms of our design. It also helps to further abstract the client-server relationship.

**Interviewer**: That's a good point. However, I don't see many candidates designing an API with one endpoint.

**Candidate**: True. But that gave us a good direction for the rest of the interview. It clarified that with our current problem scope, we only need one endpoint.

**Interviewer:** Please continue.

## Step 4: Articulate the data model

**Candidate:** With our API established, I'd like to take a look at designing a data model in order to store and handle data around this problem.

**Interviewer:** Is data storage a critical problem? I'm thinking specifically about system performance.

**Candidate:** Data storage is very important to maintain a performant system. With many different text searching algorithms, a popular data format is a trie. Tries are tree-like structures that can hold characters at each node and have children characters.

Searching for a matching string within a trie structure is fast. Its polynomial search time is $O(n)$, where n is the length of the string.

I believe using a trie in this situation is ideal. When a user types in a partial search phrase, it is much faster to search through a trie rather than linearly through an entire database. A trie can help especially with the partial search phrase.

**Interviewer:** I understand what a trie is and agree that it may be helpful here. Can you explain how we would traverse a trie, given a user's partial search term?

**Candidate:** Let's say we have the partial search phrase "ama", and the user intends to search for "amazon". While the user types in each character of "ama", our system will digest a trie, traversing the data structure for each character.

Given a sample trie and the current search phrase "ama", this is how our system would process our trie.

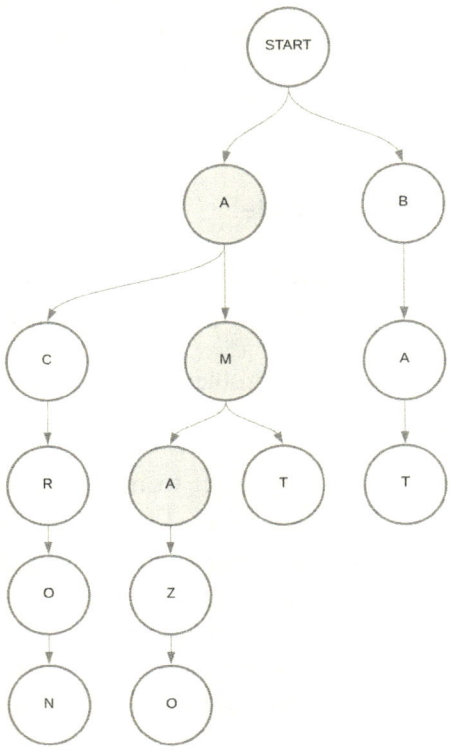

*Sample trie object*

The System Design Interview

Once it reaches the last character of the current search term, it will return the top 10 associated searches with that current search term. The node ending the term "ama" will contain the top 10 search queries with that prefix.

**Interviewer:** This makes sense. But you skipped the step in how we will not only create a trie structure but also populate each node with the Top 10 suggestions of search queries. How do we solve these issues?

**Candidate:** Correct. The general algorithm to find potential search queries is what I have described. I have yet to articulate how we will create the trie and generate predicted search terms.

Let's start by collecting data in a fashion that will allow us to have a self-updating system. We can create services that act as aggregators of data, simply calling them Aggregators. These Aggregators monitor current searches and collect metrics about them.

These Aggregators take each search term in the last hour, collect the number of times that term was searched for, and write it to a database. We can use a Cassandra NoSQL database since it is optimized for large amounts of writes. Since we are writing new search terms every hour.

| Timestamp | Term | Count |
| --- | --- | --- |
| XX/XX/XX 10:00 | AMAZON | 1928 |
| XX/XX/XX 11:00 | AMAZON | 1875 |
| XX/XX/XX 12:00 | AMAZON | 3145 |
| XX/XX/XX 13:00 | AMAZON | 2435 |
| XX/XX/XX 14:00 | AMAZON | 1241 |
| XX/XX/XX 15:00 | AMAZON | 5423 |
| XX/XX/XX 16:00 | AMAZON | 3523 |
| XX/XX/XX 17:00 | AMAZON | 989 |
| XX/XX/XX 18:00 | AMAZON | 1185 |

With all of this hourly data for search queries, other processes and services can come in and update our tries with new text paths as well as top 10 suggestions at each node. Let's call this process an Applier.

An Applier reads our Cassandra DB after each hourly write and updates our trie with updated paths as well as predictions at each node.

To outline what our Applier does:

- Reads Cassandra DB for new search terms and adds appropriate nodes to our global trie
- For each node in our trie:

- o Finds all hourly search data points with that nodes prefix
- o Calculates an importance score for each search term with that shared prefix
- o Adds the top 10 into the node of the trie so we can return it immediately

With this general algorithm, our auto-suggest service can suggest search terms.

**Interviewer:** So, you said we have two entities called Aggregators and Appliers? How do they function? Who runs them and when?

**Candidate:** Our Aggregators and Appliers can be daemon services that run in the background of our system. Our main application takes a user's partial search query and returns the top 10 search terms in the node that ends the user's partial search query.

**Interviewer:** So these are daemon services that support our overall application. They run in the background and aggregate and organize data so that all our overall application has to do is find the prefix in our trie and return the predicted search terms that are stored at that node?

**Candidate:** Exactly. That's the general concept with these components.

Since we have a general idea of how our system works, I think we'll jump into how these components interact. The best way to solve this problem is to design the system itself. That will help us sort out these detailed issues.

**Interviewer:** All right.

## Step 5: List the architectural components

**Candidate:** Right now, we have three components:

- Aggregators
- Appliers
- Application Servers

Here's a system overview:

1. We have our application server, which uses our trie object to return predicted search queries.
2. Connected to this application server is the Aggregator, which takes the final search term and collects general user activity to generate better search suggestions.
3. Lastly, we have our Applier. This Applier runs after every Aggregator dump, more as a callback service or function; it helps our system keep its data fresh by updating our system's global trie.

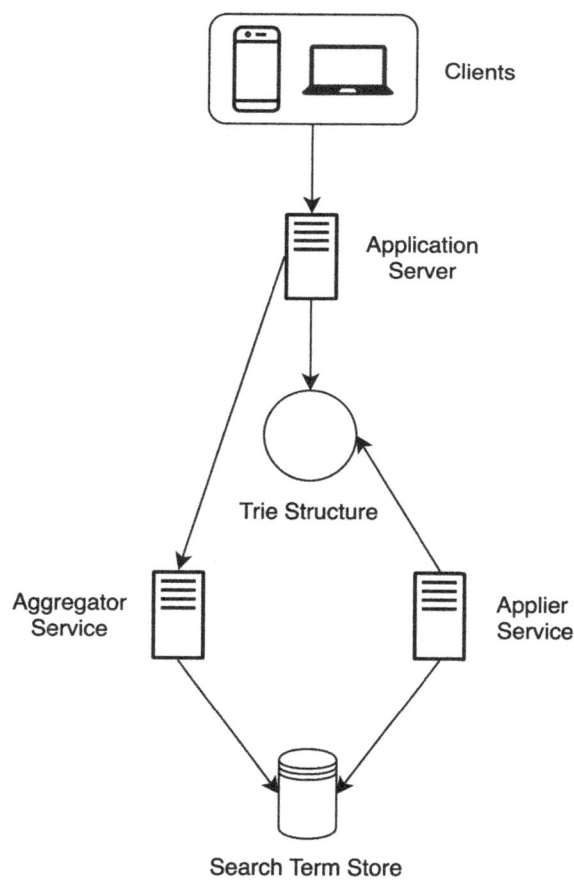

*General System Overview*

**Interviewer:** It makes more sense now that we have visualized our system architecture. Can you explain a little more how the system will work?

**Candidate:** Sure. In the situation where our system provides search suggestions to users:

- A user types in a partial search query which is the argument into our API /suggestions.
- The system searches down our trie data structure to find the terminal node of the user's current search term.
- The terminal node stores the top 10 search suggestions for that current search phrase. The suggestions are based on the previous history of search terms.
- These 10 search suggestions are returned to the user's API call, which is then abstractly displayed to the user.

In the situation where we aggregate and apply data to update our trie data structure:

- Many final search requests hit our service.
- For each hour, we aggregate these search terms into a count table within a Cassandra database.
- After our Aggregator dump, our Applier runs and calculates new metrics for each search term.
- It then generates a new trie structure and replaces the old trie so our system stays up to date with current trends.

**Interviewer:** May I ask what is the purpose of running the Applier every hour? Also, how does this help our system keep up with "current trends"?

**Candidate**: It can help keep our system up to date with trends that are occurring around the world. Let's say there's a big event, like a massive NASDAQ stock drop. Users will overwhelm our search service with the search term "NASDAQ." To reduce latency, we aggregate recent trends;

partial search terms like "NAS" may imply a full search term like "NASDAQ."

On other days, however, when there are major NASCAR racing events, "NAS" may imply a top suggestion of "NASCAR."

To recap, it helps our system dynamically keep up with trends.

**Interviewer**: Good insight. Normally with auto-suggest, we assume globally popular search trends, but this system can adapt to trends down to the hour. So why did you choose an hour as the time interval?

**Candidate**: To be honest, it was an arbitrary choice. I can think of situations where every hour is not frequent enough.

To find the optimal refresh frequency, we can run an A/B test to see which refresh frequency gives the most accurate predictions, as measured by auto-suggest click-through rate.

**Interviewer**: That's fantastic. I like your data-driven approach.

## Step 6: Scale

**Candidate:** Perfect. Now that we have a general architecture, I'd like to scale this system to meet our performance requirements.

**Interviewer:** What are the scalability weaknesses of our system so far?

**Candidate:** There are several:

- We only have one global trie that responds to all user requests.
- This can cause problems when our Applier modifies our current trie with new paths and updated predicted searches.
- We have one application server that fulfills all user requests.
- We have one trie that may not meet our performance needs.

**Interviewer:** Very good. You know what we need to improve. How would you go about addressing those weaknesses and creating a more robust system?

**Candidate**: Let's tackle each of these weaknesses individually.

Our single global trie causes many bottlenecks in our system. Although our API can support many concurrent read requests to our trie, the hourly update of our trie by the Applier can result in times when our system has no trie, causing our system to stall until the Applier is ready.

To fix this problem, we duplicate our global trie into 3 different replicas. So when the Applier updates our global trie, it does not stop incoming requests. Our Applier can update one trie at a time so there's always two available tries.

Moreover, each duplicated trie represents an immense amount of data over time. This large object can cause latency issues when traversing the trie during a prefix search. To mitigate this, we partition our trie into 3 separate tries. We can put all prefixes starting with the letters A-I, J-R, and S-Z into separate trie objects. This way, we now have 3 "sub-tries" that take care of different query ranges. In addition, all three sub-tries each have three replicas of their own.

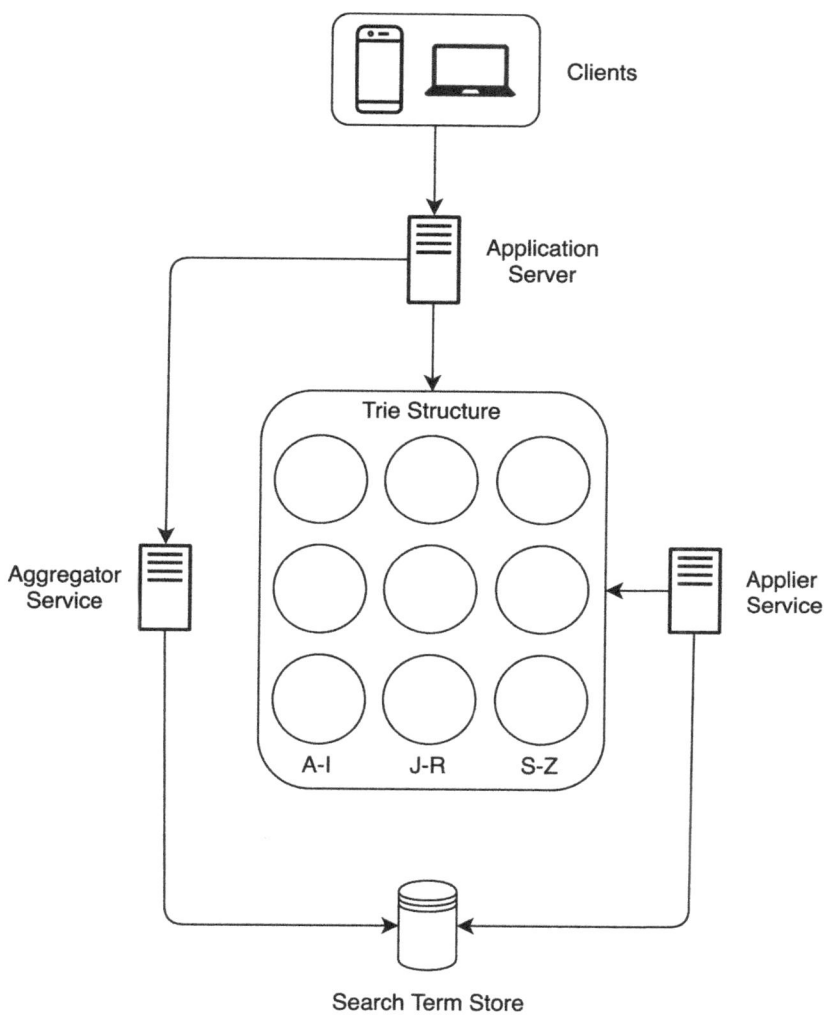

*System Overview - Trie Segmentation and Replica*

The System Design Interview

Lastly, we only have one server to handle all user requests. Let's simply scale our system with multiple servers preceded by a load balancer to distribute requests evenly.

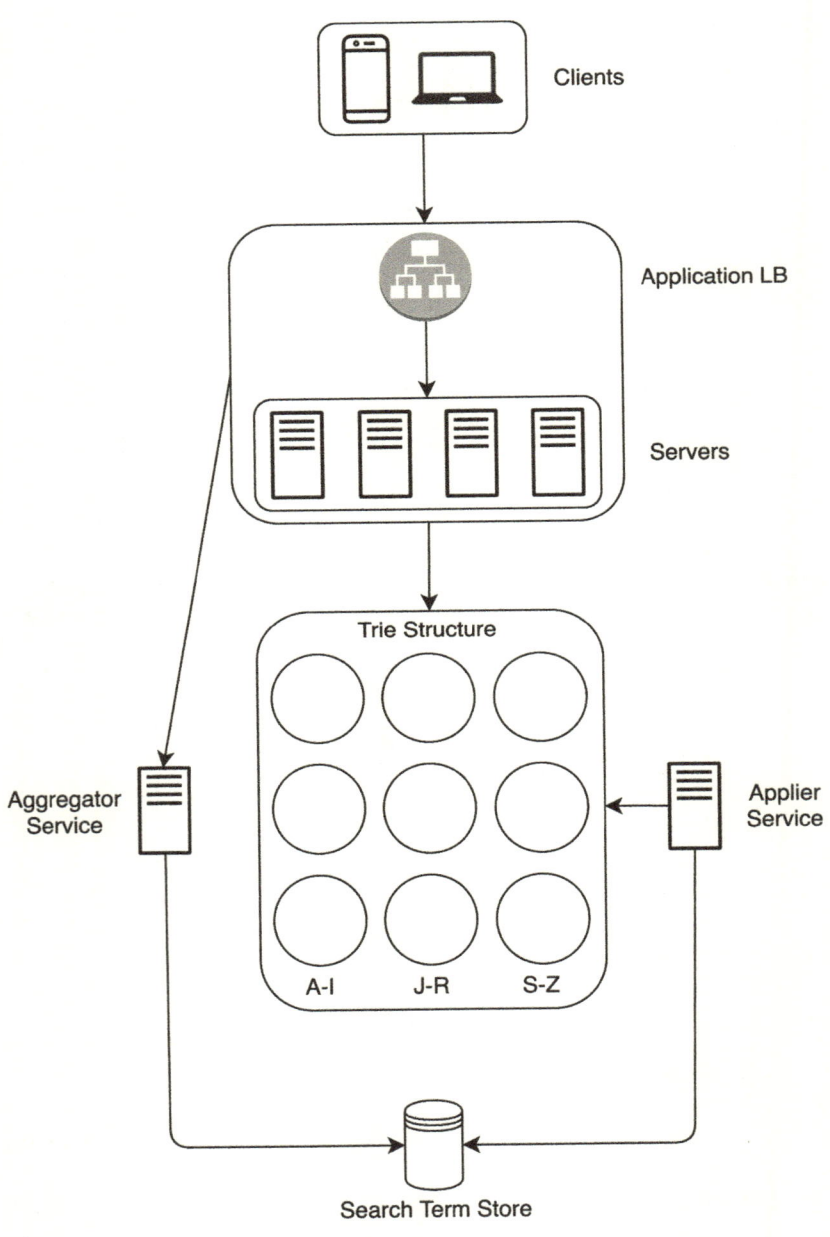

*System Overview - Load Balancer and Servers*

*The System Design Interview*

**Interviewer**: I hope you don't mind me interrupting. Given a user's partial query, how does our application server know which trie and replica to go to?

**Candidate**: There are two ways to accomplish this.

First, our application server itself can know all 9 of our trie locations. While it's the easiest solution, it can lead to some hard coding. This will increase our technical debt.

The other approach is to have an Apache Zookeeper instance. Zookeeper will return the matching trie instance based on the first character when a query is made. It can select a random replica from the subset of replicas that match the first character. This should result in an even distribution of reads across all replicas.

The second approach is much better in terms of clean design and eliminating potential technical debt during development.

**Interviewer**: Very good. I think the second approach is the one we should take.

What other areas of improvement can we take?

**Candidate**: I see that we can extend our general Aggregators and Appliers to better handle continuous requests from users. It would be beneficial if we had an Applier for each alphabetic subdomain that our system handles. Similarly, having Cassandra databases for each alphabetic set of tries can reduce the load on our system.

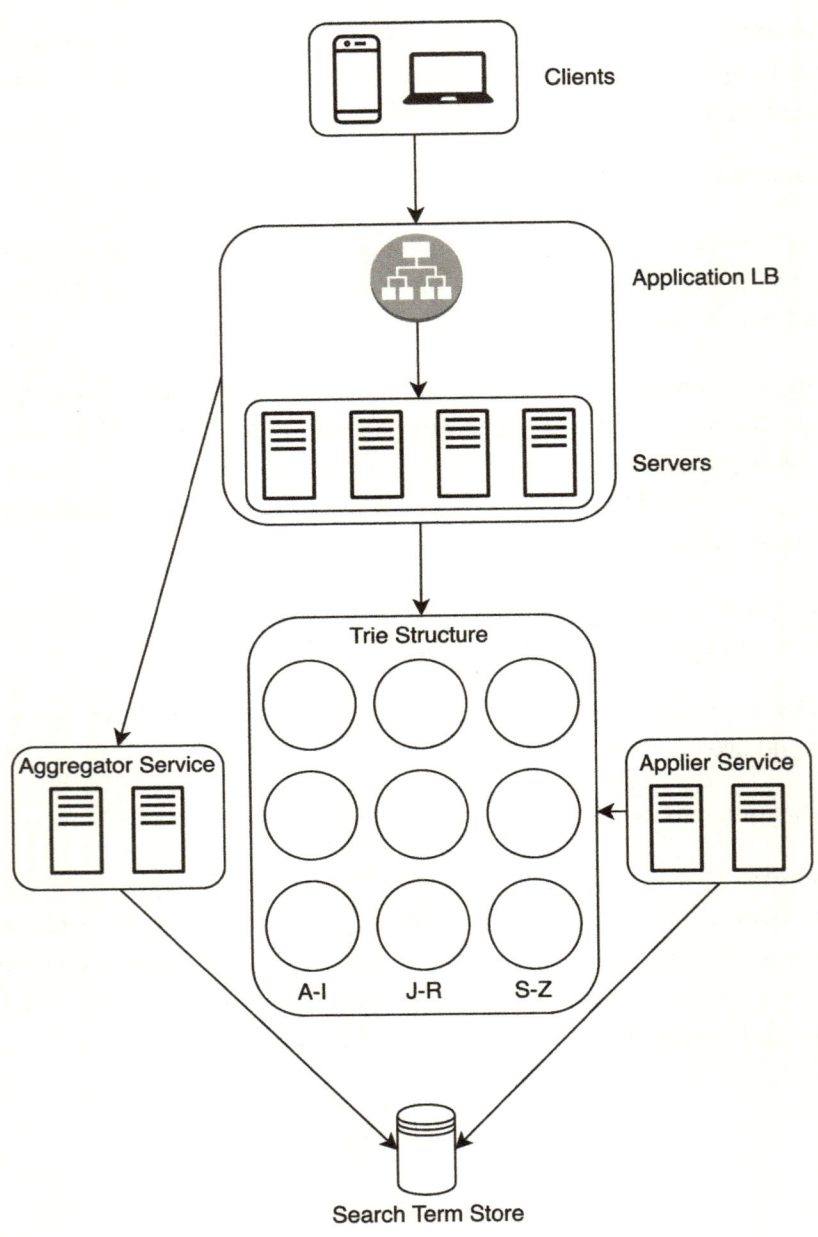

*System Overview - Fully Scaled*

*The System Design Interview*

**Interviewer:** This solution seems to scale efficiently, and we have used testing frameworks to adjust some parameters of our system once in production, which is fantastic. Currently, our system should be able to address all our capacity estimations. Lastly, it looks like we are running short on time.

**Candidate:** Alright. Did you have any questions for me regarding my thought process or design decisions?

**Interviewer:** Yeah. Specifically, why did you decide to create these Appliers? How did you come about this workflow to generate suggestions?

**Candidate:** I believe following a user-focused strategy is optimal to design this system. Having the ability to change our suggestions based on current user trends as well as standard suggestions allows for a powerful system that will produce impactful results.

I don't see value in a system that generates simple suggestions that may not be of value to users.

**Interviewer:** That's great you are focused on the impact our product will have on users. Usually, candidates seem to be satisfied with a more general approach that does not address fine-tuned issues that could bolster the product.

**Candidate:** Thanks! Did you have any other questions for me regarding this problem?

**Interviewer:** Nope. Looks like you did a good job thoroughly explaining your thought process and being able to focus on the user. Great job!

# Design an Air Traffic Controller

**Things to Consider**
- Unpredictable traffic flow due to delays
- Bottlenecks like the limited number of available gates
- Constraints like circling planes that may run out of fuel

**Mistakes to Avoid**
- Thinking that the interviewer isn't interested in discussing algorithms for a system design question
- Assuming that all data must be retained forever
- Assuming that an air traffic system should adopt the same system architecture as popular Internet applications

**Interviewer**: Good afternoon! Welcome to our company. I'd like to go over an interesting system design problem.

**Candidate**: Good day to you as well. What is the problem?

**Interviewer**: Usually, system design interviews are more about the main pillars of system architecture and scalability and not algorithmic thinking. Today I wanted to solve a problem that focused on algorithms and critical thinking.

I don't want the solution to this problem to be 100% technically driven and outlined. Rather, I want a discussion about how we can design this system.

The goal of this conversation is to discuss the design of an air traffic control system.

**Candidate**: What exactly is the primary goal of the air traffic control system? What is it designed to accomplish?

**Interviewer**: The system focuses on tracking and managing the number of aircraft on the runways and taxiing traffic. Air traffic controllers can use this system to direct aircraft onto the tarmac. Does that make sense? We want to curb the number of aircraft on the runway and keep it manageable for the controllers.

**Candidate**: That makes sense. When you curb the number of aircraft on the tarmac, do you mean all aspects like leaving the gates, taking off, and landing? That is, do we want to maintain a reasonably constant number of aircraft regardless of where they are on the tarmac?

**Interviewer**: Exactly. We want to make it easier for the controllers; their jobs can be very stressful.

**Candidate**: All right. What limit should we be aiming for?

**Interviewer**: It depends on the airport and its capacity. For now, we limit our airport to 15 aircraft on the tarmac at any one time. Ideally, our system should be able to work with any value within that limit.

**Candidate**: So, if there are 15 aircraft on the tarmac at any given time, we reject incoming landing requests?

**Interviewer**: That's right. When we reach that threshold, we deny all takeoff, landing, and gate departure requests.

**Candidate**: Should we split our total capacity into departing and landing capacity? For instance, landing aircraft should have a different priority than departing aircraft. Prioritizing both equally can cause congestion on the tarmac.

**Interviewer**: In theory, this sounds like a solid plan, but how would you balance the capacity of landing aircraft versus departing aircraft?

**Candidate**: Well, we want to make sure we don't clog the tarmac with arriving aircraft. To do this, we should allocate roughly 35 to 45 percent of the total capacity to arriving aircraft and the rest to departing aircraft. Since we have a total capacity of 15 aircraft, let's split it into 6 arriving aircraft to 9 departing aircraft.

**Interviewer**: I like this strategy.

**Candidate**: What about the situation where an airport might have an emergency landing? I don't think we can turn down such requests. How should we respond to that?

**Interviewer**: That's an interesting point. What is an appropriate action in that scenario?

**Candidate**: Okay. I think ironing out core functionality should happen before backup or emergency situations. I'll come back to that issue later in the process.

Let's get to the other gray areas of this question. How does our system know all the departures and arrivals on the schedule?

**Interviewer**: Let's say the airport provides a service that shares the current day's departures and arrivals. However, the provided data are simply estimates. The real operating hours differ from the schedule.

**Candidate**: All right. Let's tackle some estimates that we need to take care of in this prompt. How often will our system encounter departure and arrival events? What is the average time between events like takeoffs and landings?

**Interviewer**: I would say this airport has a median of one takeoff or landing every 50-70 seconds.

**Candidate**: With planes taking off or landing every minute, how many planes are on the ground in a single moment?

**Interviewer**: Let's assume that we have about 70 planes at the airport at any one time.

**Candidate**: All right. These estimates give us an idea of the demand requirements. Let's try to design an initial version.

I wanted to start by outlining an API that can serve as a guide for developing our system. This API can serve as a guide to the functionality of what our system can do.

**Interviewer**: That's a great idea. What does this API involve?

**Candidate**: Setting up the appropriate endpoints through which our system can interact will help us define our feature set.

**Interviewer**: Good. What kind of endpoints do you want to create?

**Candidate**: Let's look at the functionality of our air traffic system. It basically controls how many planes can be on the tarmac at one time.

There are several ways that aircraft can request to be placed on the tarmac.

They can ask for a departure permit, a takeoff permit, a landing permit, or a docking permit at the gate. These four critical steps are important to get a fixed number of aircraft.

In turn, let's create API endpoints for each of these approval checks to ensure that our system can approve and deny permits at each stage:

| API Endpoint | Description | Arguments |
| --- | --- | --- |
| /gateDepart | Request to depart a gate | Flight No., Gate |
| /takeOff | Request to takeoff | Flight No., Runway |
| /land | Request to land | Flight No., Runway |
| /gateDock | Request to dock at a gate | Flight No., Gate |
| /emergencyLand | Request to make an emergency landing | Flight No. |

Let me know if I'm missing anything. Otherwise, we can move to define the datastore and system design.

**Interviewer**: I like how your API endpoints map elegantly to the typical actions of an air traffic system. Please continue.

**Candidate**: Thank you! It seemed logical to express each system function as a single endpoint.

Moving on, data storage will be tricky. We need to track the number of planes waiting to:

1. Gate Depart
2. Take Off
3. Land
4. Gate Dock

Each one of these elements should have a wait queue.

**Interviewer**: Got it. But how do we know how many aircraft are on the tarmac at the current time? Obviously, if the tarmac is free, we can permit planes out of those queues.

**Candidate**: We can have a single, global counter that tracks the number of aircraft on the tarmac.

**Interviewer**: Very good. That's a good solution. Are there any problems you see with the current layout with four queues?

**Candidate**: Well, my only concern is how we're going to prioritize those queues. For example, if we have a single airplane in all four queues, which one do we release first?

We can address that by thinking critically about what is most optimal for the airport. If we allow a plane to land, it will add more congestion to our gate dock queue.

result in increased congestion that would clog our gate queue. I don't think that path is appropriate.

On the other hand, if we allow takeoffs first, our tarmac will clear faster. Planes can land and then dock at gates. I think this solution is more optimal.

Let's prioritize the queues as follows, starting with the most important first:

1. Take Off
2. Gate Depart
3. Gate Dock
4. Land

**Interviewer**: Giving the lowest priority to the landing planes seems counterintuitive to me. What if they run out of fuel?

**Candidate**: Landing planes need to dock quickly at free gates. If there aren't any free gates, there's no reason for them to land and clog the tarmac. Jamming the tarmac can prevent planes from departing the gates and taking off, making the situation worse.

**Interviewer**: Now that you put it that way that does make sense. Please continue.

**Candidate**: I don't believe a database is the best way to store the queues. The queues are live data that doesn't need to persist beyond a single day's activity, right? If that's the case, then we can just store the queues in system memory.

Similarly, the airport's scheduled departures and arrivals need to be stored in a database. At the beginning of each morning, we can populate a local table with the data provided by the airport service with the scheduled departures and arrivals.

We can use these scheduled activities to better manage traffic.

**Interviewer**: I understand that you keep the queues in the system memory since it is live data. But how does it make sense to keep the scheduled departures and arrivals in a database?

**Candidate**: Depending on the activity level of the day, it is safe to store them in a local database table that can be deleted at the end of each day.

We can use this database with certain heuristics to adjust the performance of our system. For example, if we query our database for the next hour and find that the majority of activity is arrivals, we would emphasize our departures and arrivals activity to ensure that we have enough free gates. Does that make sense?

**Interviewer**: Yes, I see your point. However, you have 4 different queues in local storage. How are you going to address each queue separately but with a consistent priority?

**Candidate**: In many computing topics, we can use priority queues and time blocks. To explain this further, we can set up each queue type to order events by time, right?

From here, our air traffic system will only respond to one queue: a merged version of all queues. We can merge the queues by comparing activities based on time intervals. Instead of comparing direct times, we compare the 5- to 10-minute intervals in which they were placed. We separate the event timestamp into 5 to 10-minute time intervals.

For example, if we have a takeoff request at 10:08 and a landing request at 10:05, we would satisfy the takeoff request first. Since both requests are in the 5-minute time block 10:05-10:10, they are treated the same. Also, take-off events have a higher priority in our system; therefore, the take-off event would be fulfilled first.

**Interviewer**: That's an interesting approach. I like the concept, but what about time sensitivity? Airports are busy centers of activity. Wouldn't aggregating requests into 10-minute intervals reduce airport efficiency?

**Candidate**: I agree, 10-minute intervals may not be the best. Instead, we can experiment with time window duration.

**Interviewer**: What do you mean by experimenting with time windows?

**Candidate**: We can run A/B tests with different time window durations. Each airport is unique; they support different traffic volumes and patterns. It would be best to find an optimal value for each airport; a fixed time window does not fit all.

**Interviewer**: Excellent. That's a great way to reduce that uncertainty. So, to recap, what does your system look like right now?

**Candidate**: First of all, we have our API endpoints that take care of the various functions in our system. These endpoints respond to planes that:

1. Take Off
2. Gate Depart
3. Gate Dock
4. Land

Moving on to the internal data store for our system. Pending requests are stored in queues depending on the request type. On the other hand, scheduled arrivals and departures are stored in a local database table so that our system can query the next X scheduled operations to adjust its performance.

**Interviewer**: I see. That makes sense so far. What are we missing now to complete our system design and work out the specifics?

**Candidate**: We should design the physical system.

**Interviewer**: Right. What physical components would we need for this system?

**Candidate**: Our system does not need to cater to millions of users making billions of requests.

Therefore, a standard server-database relationship is sufficient for a functional system. It meets our need for a server that can handle many incoming requests and store the current day's scheduled activities.

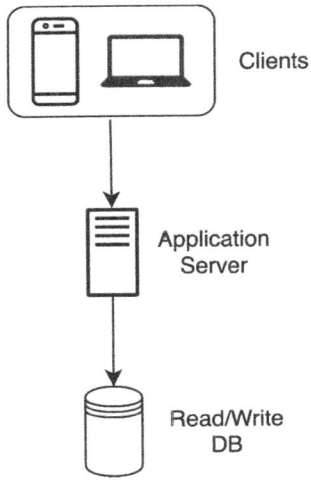

*The System Design Interview*

**Interviewer**: Are there any vulnerabilities in this standard server and database relationship?

**Candidate**: I do think that our system could benefit from improved failover. We can also use logging for error reporting.

**Interviewer**: How would you solve these problems?

**Candidate**: For failover, I would recommend a separate file storage system for our live queues. We can always have a backup queue written to disk to ensure that our requests are not lost in the event of a failure.

For logging, we can use standard logging frameworks to record events such as requests received, responses sent, and take-off events. In fact, in the long run, this logging can help us find optimal hyperparameters for our system, such as the size of the time interval. We can store our logs in our server's file storage alongside the backup queue files.

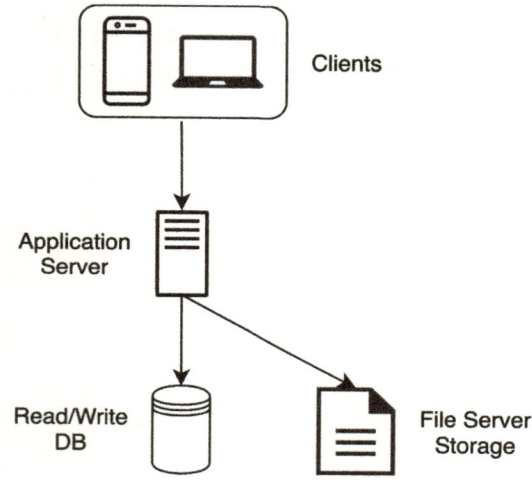

*The System Design Interview*

**Interviewer**: Those are great adjustments to make sure the system is robust.

**Candidate**: Next, I wanted to consider scalability.

I know this system doesn't need extensive scalability because it doesn't respond to millions of devices or store petabytes of data. However, to be highly responsive, the system needs to take into account the number of active connections.

Since it is not a distributed system, we can scale our server vertically to handle more active connections.

**Interviewer**: Perfect! That's a great way to make sure our system meets scalability requirements.

**Candidate**: Exactly. With all that said, I believe our system is functional and stable. Do you have any other questions?

**Interviewer**: No, I don't think so. I liked your thoughtful response and your willingness to go into the details.

**Candidate**: Thank you very much.

# Chapter 11 Concepts You Should Know

This chapter contains detailed yet succinct explanations for technical concepts you'll encounter in the system design interview.

## Service Design and APIs

Here are some concepts you should know related to service design and APIs. It maps closely with the third step of the PEDALS framework, Design the Service.

### Application Programming Interface (API)

API is an acronym that stands for application programming interface.

An API exposes programming functions to third-party developers. These developers can incorporate and execute those functions in their code. These third-party developers cannot see or change how the underlying functions are implemented.

For example, a ride-sharing app can request and display map data via the Google Maps API.

### REST APIs

REST stands for Representational State Transfer. REST is a way for two systems to communicate over HTTP, similar to how web browsers communicate with servers.

REST API is an important standard when exchanging information between two systems. Other standards, like SOAP, were unnecessarily complex and arbitrary.

An API is called a REST API or RESTful API when it follows these six design principles:

1. **Client-Server Architecture.** A client can make requests to the server using an interface.
2. **Stateless.** Every API request and response contain all the necessary information to compute results without relying on state elements.

3. **Cacheable**. The data transfer between clients and server must be cacheable.
4. **Uniform Interface**. The client only needs to know the immediate layer its interfacing with, allowing the application and API to grow independently.
5. **Layered System**. API is designed in a layered and hierarchal manner, making it organized and modular.
6. **Code on Demand**. The server can extend a client app on run time.

RESTful API typically use standard HTTP verbs such as:

- `GET` - retrieves information from a server
- `POST` - writes new information to a server
- `PUT` - updates prior information to a server
- `DELETE` - removes information from a server

## Atomic Operations

Atomic operations can't be partially executed. Once triggered, they must complete.

## Backpressure

In fluid dynamics, backpressure is a term that describes a resistant force against the normal flow of fluid through a pipe. In the software world, data flows through workflows throughout production systems.

In this context, backpressure describes events or operations that resist the flow of data through a system. For example, I/O operations break the execution flow of systems, which creates backpressure for incoming data that requires processing.

## Callback Functions

A callback function is a function that's executed after another function completes.

For example, an e-commerce site may direct a 3rd-party payment system make a call to the e-commerce site's thank you page after a credit card transaction has been processed.

## Concurrency

Concurrency allows different parts of a program to run at the same time without affecting the outcome (in a negative way).

Here's an example from banking. Let's say a couple shares a bank account. They both decide to withdraw $500 at the same time, but they only have $750 in their account. Concurrency ensures that the couple doesn't overdraw their account.

There are three common tactics to ensure concurrency:

- Locking
- Atomicity
- Transactions

### Locking

Locking is a mechanism where a process has the right to update or write data. When a process acquires a lock, other processes cannot update or write data.

Going back to our banking example, let's say one person starts process A and the other starts process B.

- Process A acquires the lock, allowing it to manipulate account data. It successfully retrieves that lock and withdraws money.
- Process B attempts to acquire the lock for the bank account. The lock is being used by process A, so process B is put on the lock waitlist.
- Process A withdraws $500, leaving $250 in the account. Process A releases the lock.
- Process B successfully gets the lock and attempts to withdrawn $500.
- The request is rejected because there is only $250 left.

## Atomic

An atomic action is an action whose intermediate state cannot be seen by other processes or threads.

Going back to our banking example, let's say process A debits $500 from the account. However, an ATM error, after the debit, resulted in the user not getting the cash. (Perhaps the ATM lost power.)

If process B was able to see the intermediate state, it may have wrongly assumed that the $500 already left the account. However, if the system was designed with atomicity in mind, process B wouldn't be able to see this intermediate state.

## Transactions

A transaction is a sequence of atomic operations.

With our banking example, we would need the entire sequence of debiting cash – updating the account, releasing funds via ATM – to be atomic. Doing so would make it clear the withdrawal was not incomplete.

# Containers

A container is a unit of software that packages code and its dependencies so it can run in any computing environment like Linux or Windows.

The biggest benefit of containers is that it allows the software to run consistently from one environment to another. Thanks to containers, developers spend less time debugging and diagnosing how underlying differing environments affect how their code is run.

Docker is the most popular container technology today. Software that is contained in Docker is called a Docker image.

Kubernetes is a container orchestration system. Without Kubernetes, developers would have to write scripts for their deployment workflows. Kubernetes helps developers schedule and scale their Docker containers.

# Daemon Services

Daemon services are background processes.

For example, a daemon can be set up to:

- Pre-compute results, such as one's newsfeed, to speed up response time
- Re-train an ML model using new data

Daemon stands for **D**isk **A**nd **E**xecution **MON**itor.

## Fan Out

Fan out describes a messaging strategy that delivers a message to multiple destinations without burdening the sender. Fan out typically happens in parallel, and the process does not halt or wait for responses to their message.

## Event-Driven Programming

Event-driven programming is when the program flow is driven by the user or program events.

For example, when a user stops typing in the search box, it triggers a request for auto-complete suggestions.

## Hashing

Hashing is an algorithm that takes a key and converts it into a unique value. The inputs can be of various sizes, and the output is a unique, fixed-size id ("hash").

A perfect hashing algorithm has the following characteristics:

- *Uniformity*. Generates a unique hash for every distinct value.
- *Stability*. Always generates the same hash for the same input.
- *Continuity*. If used for sorting or searching, the algorithm produces similar hashes for similar items.
- *Non-invertible*. The algorithm is one-way; the original input cannot be determined by the hash. This is especially for cryptography purposes.

You might use hashes for:

- Hashing a password before storing it in a database. This provides more security and allows a constant-sized password field in the database. MD5 and SHA are two popular hashing algorithms used for cryptographic purposes.
- A URL shortening service. For example, the bit.ly service turns *www.example.com* into the shortened URL, *bit.ly/1h0ceQI,* using a hashing algorithm.
- Hash tables are a common data structure that chooses memory storage locations using a hash. This allows objects to be stored and retrieved quickly and efficiently.

## JSON

*See serialization.*

## Locality

Locality is the universal tendency that a processor, via the application, is likely to:

1. Access the same storage location soon
2. Access adjacent storage soon

The first concept is called temporal locality and the second concept is called spatial locality.

System designers can optimize systems to account for locality; the most common locality optimization is utilizing a cache.

*See caching.*

## Logical Design

A system's logical design is an abstract representation of its data flows. This includes a description of:

- Inputs
- Outputs
- Datastores
- Data flows

A logical design doesn't specify the hardware or architectural requirements, but the physical design does.

## Machine Learning

Machine learning refers to algorithms that perform tasks based on *inference* rather than *rules*.

These inferences are derived from mathematical models that "learn" from large amounts of structured data.

For example, a developer can create a music recommendation service based on rules. For example, we can program an *explicit* rule that says if a user likes artist A then recommend music from artist B.

Machine learning is different. Instead, a machine learning algorithm will be given training data. Based on that training data, the algorithm will *infer* the data points that predict a particular outcome.

Example of provided data, for a music recommendation service, can include:

- **Listening history**. Users who listen to a song are likely to listen to another song. This is called collaborative filtering.
- **Keywords**. The song's metadata or lyrics can provide clues. For example, the song's metadata might indicate that the song is appropriate for toddlers. Or the song lyrics might indicate that the song is related to New York.
- **Audio file analysis**. The music recommendation service might analyze the song file's characteristics including tempo, loudness, key, and time signature.

Other popular applications of machine learning include:

- Fraud detection
- Self-driving cars
- Voice recognition
- Email spam detection
- Shopping and movie recommendations

## Features

A feature is a property of an event, observation, or data point. Here are some examples:

- For a music recommendation, a song's tempo combined with the genre may accurately predict the music one would like.
- In email spam detection, the word "FREE" in the subject line may more accurately predict spam.
- In e-commerce, whether a user using an Apple device, may more accurately predict how likely that user will make a purchase.

Choosing features is very important. It can significantly impact prediction accuracy.

## Training Data

Training data, as the name implies, is data that trains machine learning models.

## Validation Data

After a machine learning model has been trained, the validation data set is processed to gauge the machine learning model's accuracy.

## Supervised vs. Unsupervised Learning

Supervised learning is a machine learning model that makes predictions (output) with clear inputs.

Unsupervised learning is a machine learning model that makes predictions (output) with unclear inputs.

For example, a self-driving car application may be given a clear (labeled) input that certain intersections have red stop signs. Based on this labeled data, the machine learning algorithm can infer that cars should stop when it encounters intersections with stop signs. This is an example of supervised learning.

However, a self-driving car application may not be given labeled data indicating which intersections have red stop signs. Instead, it would have to infer from the data available to it, when the car should stop. For example, it may wrongly infer that:

- **Stop**: When it approaches an intersection and other cars are slowing down.
- **Not stop**: When it approaches an intersection and other cars aren't present.

### Neural Networks
A neural network is another learning model. Just like machine learning, it learns without specific rules.

A neural network model process signals (i.e. data) like neurons in the human brain. A specific neuron can signal other neurons it is connected to.

### Batching
The concept of aggregating portions of the training data together. These aggregations are "learned" together, instead of one by one. Batching training data reduces the number of times gradients are calculated to adjust weights through backpropagation.

### Deep Learning
Group of machine learning methods that are fundamentally based on neural networks. This includes variations of neural networks such as recurrent neural networks (RNNs) and convolutional neural networks (CNNs).

## Message Queues
Queues are a component of some service-based architectures. Queues accept client messages for delivery to a service, then hold the message until the service requests delivery.

Once a queue has accepted a message, it provides a strong guarantee that the message will *eventually* be read and processed.

Messages remain in the queue and available for delivery until the server confirms that it has finished with the message and deletes it.

Messages in queues will be delivered *at least once*, so they may be delivered *more than once*. It's important to have unique identifiers on the messages to prevent unwanted duplicate actions such as purchases.

Here's an example of a typical queue interaction:

- A message is put into the queue by the client. (Click "Buy" on Amazon)
- The queue confirms it has received the message. ("Thank you for your order!" page)
- The server requests a batch of messages from the queue.
- The server processes the messages. (Charge credit card; send "Your Amazon Order Confirmation" email)
- The server asks the queue to delete the processed messages by id.

Messaging queues are also called message brokers or queuing service. Some of the popular message queues include RabbitMQ and AWS SQS.

Queues are often themselves microservices with a load balancer, persistence, and redundancy.

Queues may also offer a pub/sub (publisher/subscriber) model.

- This allows multiple services to consume a message from a single service.
- Each subscriber is given a queue.
- New subscribers can be added without the need to update the publishing service.

You might use queues or pub/sub to:

- **Help your service scale**. Especially if traffic has occasional large spikes a queue can let your servers handle traffic as fast as they can leading to delayed responses instead of a total crash.
- **Reliably pass messages between microservices**. Even if one service breaks down, the rest of the system can keep working around the failure without data loss.

- **Add eventual consistency to your system.** Because we can't be consistent, available, and distributed at the same time, relaxing consistency is usually the right choice.
- **Search result suggestions.** A partial search string can be sent after every keystroke. If the user pauses, the results have time to arrive and be displayed.
- **Allowing access to your data stream for BI, machine learning, analytics, or database mirroring.** Instead of directly writing to the database, write events can be published and delivered to the DB and any other subscribers. New subscribing services can be added without extra work, and without adding any load to the main database.

## Microservice Architecture

Also called microservices, microservice architecture is an application designed with loosely coupled services or submodules. Here's an example:

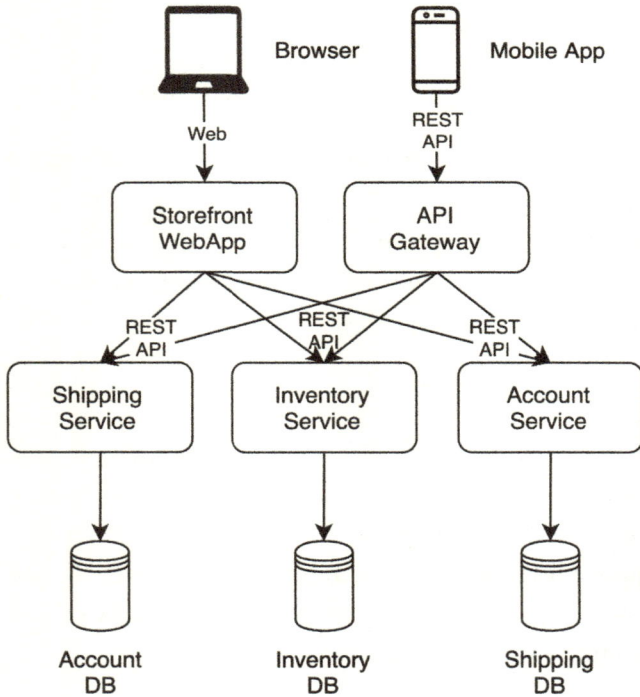

These loosely coupled services make it easy to develop and run them independently. This makes it easier to maintain, test, and scale. These microservices can even be running in different programming languages.

This is considered better than a monolithic application, which is developed from start to finish as a single unit. Monolithic applications are typically poorly organized, making it hard to debug, maintain, or extend.

## Natural Language Processing

Natural Language Processing, or NLP, refers to an application's ability to analyze, understand, and imitate human text.

## Pipeline

Pipeline refers to a chain of elements, such as processes or threads, where the output of each element is the input for the next.

Pipeline refers to a chain of elements where the output of each system process is the input for the next.

For example, we could have a pipeline consisting of two processes:

1. Sort a list alphabetically THEN
2. Output the result to a text file

Pipeline is often mentioned with a popular design strategy called pipe-and-filter, which is inspired by UNIX's pipe command.

## Polling

Checking whether another service needs attention or processing.

## Postman

Postman is a platform to assist in defining, developing, testing, and monitoring APIs.

# Proxies

## Proxy

A proxy is a server that acts as a middleman between client devices and servers of websites or companies. This proxy server intercepts requests from client devices and forwards them to the intended server.

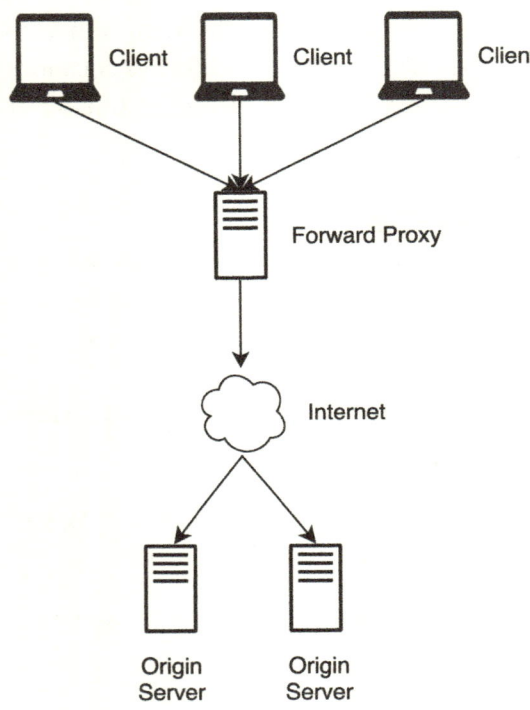

*The System Design Interview*

So why use a proxy server? There are a few reasons:

**Avoid government restrictions**
Some governments restrict internet access to certain websites. Having a proxy server to fetch the data for clients can work around that constraint.

**Enforce certain restrictions**
On the flip side, networks can direct all traffic through a proxy so certain web services can be filtered. For example, certain public schools use proxies to filter out specific web services such as pornography.

**Anonymize client device**

Since proxies do not reveal the true IP address of the client receiving the information, servers cannot identify who requested information from servers. This helps users anonymize themselves.

## Reverse Proxy

A reverse proxy is like a normal proxy but with a slight variation.

Normal proxy servers sit in front of client devices. Client devices send their requests for other servers to the proxy. Then, these proxies send requests directly to servers.

On the flip side, reverse proxies sit on the other side of the equation. Clients all request data from a server, but the server they request data from is a single reverse proxy server. This reverse proxy does not actually compute the responses for those requests. The reverse proxies forward these requests to one of many actual origin servers.

Reverse proxies allow organizations to avoid clients directly requesting information from origin servers themselves, protecting the origin servers.

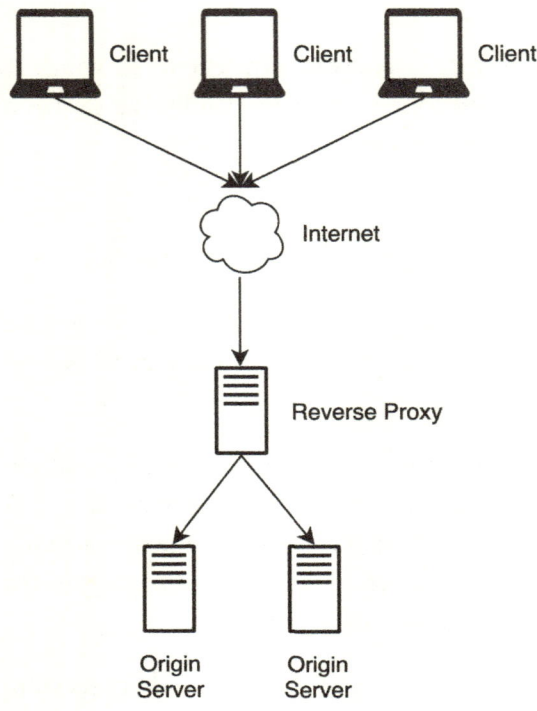

*The System Design Interview*

Why use a reverse proxy? Here are three reasons:

**Security**
Clients request data from a guarding reverse proxy server, so the locations of your company's servers aren't exposed.

Safeguarding server locations protect them from security attacks.

**Load Balancing**
Reverse proxies can balance system load, keeping systems highly performant.

**Caching**
Reverse proxy servers can cache the most common requests, preserving system resources.

## Publish and Subscribe

Publish and subscribe is a design pattern where message senders (publishers) do not specify recipients. Instead, broadcast messages without knowing the recipients. Recipients choose which messages to listen to by subscribing to specific publishers or published feeds.

Subscribers are sometimes referred to as listeners or observers.

## Remote Procedure Calls

Remote procedure calls (RPCs) trigger a subroutine on another machine, typically in the same, shared network.

The subroutine that runs on the other machine runs as if it is a local procedure call, without any knowledge it was invoked externally.

## Serialization

Serialization is about encoding data, in a specialized format, so it can be stored or transmitted; serialization allows data to be usable across different systems.

SQL is a serialization format for relational databases. JSON, XML, and CSV are other serialization formats with JSON being the most popular for web applications. Here's an example of data serialized in JSON:

```
{
    "name": "Michael Jordan",
    "team": "Chicago Bulls",
    "championships": "6"
}
```

## Software Development Kit (SDK)

SDK is a set of software tools to create applications for specific platforms.

For example, the iOS SDK is a set of tools to create an iOS app. It includes various things including:

- Libraries
- Documentation

- Code samples
- Processes
- Guides

## Stack vs. Heap

When stack and heap are mentioned together, they usually refer to a method of memory allocation. Stack *memory allocation* can be confused with stack *data structures*.

Values stored on a *stack* are deleted automatically when a function call ends.

Values stored on a *heap* are stored permanently and must be deleted manually.

## Stacks vs. Queues

Stacks and queues are popular data structures.

### Stacks

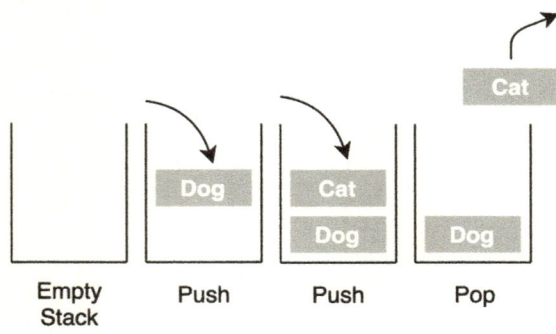

*The System Design Interview*

In a stack, new elements are added to the top of the data structure (called a "push") and elements are removed from the top of the data structure as well (called a "pop"). Stacks are also called LIFO (last in, first out) data structures due to their push and pop nature.

## Queues

*The System Design Interview*

In a queue, new elements are added to the *back* of the data structure. Elements are then removed from the *front* of the data structure. Queues are also called FIFO (first in, first out) due to their operational nature.

## Tech Debt

Implementing a technical solution with a short-term payoff (a quick fix solution) which will result in more (and substantial) work in the future. This future work is referred to as tech debt.

A quick fix typically meets a short-term need but is lacking in some way. For example, a quick fix might not handle more than 1,000 users.

Usually, when tech debt does not get paid off soon, it will only get harder to fix the software in the long-term.

## XML

*See serialization.*

# Databases, data storage, and data models

Here are some concepts you should know related to databases, data storage, and data models. It maps closely with the fourth step of the PEDALS framework, Articulate the data model.

## ACID

ACID is a set of principles for database transactions. These principles ensure data integrity in the event of a system failure, like power loss or equipment failure.

The acronym stands for:

| Property | Definition |
|---|---|
| Atomicity | Transactions will happen or not. |
| Consistency | Transactions will never leave your database in a partially complete state. |
| Isolation | Transactions are independent and separated until they're complete. |
| Durability | Any data that's already been written to the database will never be lost. |

## Apache Cassandra

Apache Cassandra is an open-source NoSQL database. Unlike other NoSQL databases like MongoDB, Cassandra is known for:

- Fast writes
- Massive scalability
- No single point of failure
- Simpler to set up in a multi-server configuration

## CAP Theorem

The CAP in CAP theorem stands for consistency, availability, and partition.

### CAP Definitions

#### Consistency
Data is the same across all components of the system. Changes within data are reflected immediately; there are no discrepancies between data values.

#### Availability
The ability for the system to be unwaveringly operational and responsive.

#### Partition Tolerance
The system continues to operate with communication breaks between system and data partitions.

### Why CAP Is Important
The CAP theorem states that between consistency, availability, and partition tolerance, a system may possess at most two traits simultaneously.

However, in practice, any system complicated enough to warrant system design will need to be able to scale onto multiple machines, so partition tolerance is almost always a given.

This leaves a choice between *consistency* and *availability*. In a perfect world, we would have all three, but a choice must be made. Consistency and availability tradeoffs can be made independently for different services within a microservice-based system architecture. That is those microservices can choose to emphasize consistency and availability, depending on their goals.

### Example CAP Theorem Tradeoffs

|  | Emphasis | Why |
| --- | --- | --- |
| Search Engine | Availability | Older search results are tolerable. It's better than making the user wait. |
| Banking apps | Consistency | Inaccurate data is unacceptable. The system cannot allow money to be overdrawn or spent twice. |
| Concert ticket sales | Consistency | It's not acceptable to sell the same concert ticket twice. |
| Airfare search | Availability | It's acceptable to indicate a particular route to be available, only to indicate during checkout that route has a different price or is no longer available for purchase.<br><br>It's near impossible to show 100% accurate data given the number of people searching around the world AND the computational complexity from calculating all possible combinations. |

Impatient users have emphasized the importance of quick results (availability) over accurate results (consistency). For example, a developer may choose to quickly load partial results (availability) and load complete results later (consistency). We call this eventual consistency.

## Database Index

A database index, or index, is a data structure that makes it fast to retrieve data from a database. That index is typically a self-balancing binary search tree where each row in a table corresponds to a tree node.

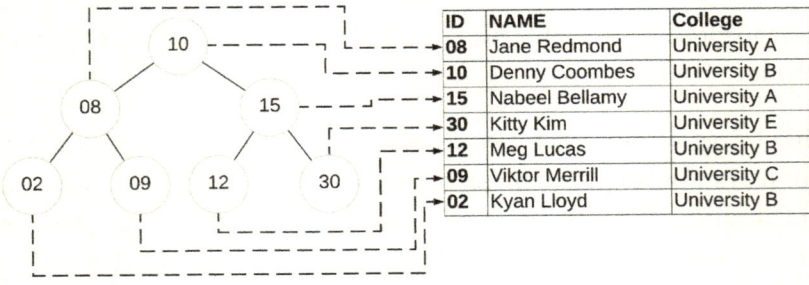

*DB Indices Tree (Left) mapped to Table Rows (Right)*

Lookups with a self-balancing binary search tree are O(log n) vs. O(n) without one.

## Eventual Consistency

Eventual consistency ensures that data across all the replicas will be consistent eventually.

You can think of eventual consistency as a property of distributed systems.

How long it takes for a distributed system to be eventually consistent is defined by the developer.

## Flat File

Flat file storage is storing data on a file like "example.txt."

Flat files are most commonly used to store:

- Configuration data
- Program constants
- Credentials
- Logs

Flat files have the advantage of taking up less space. However, flat files aren't usually structured which means their query performance is inferior to structured data stores like SQL databases.

## Object Storage

Object storage, sometimes called blob storage, works best for larger objects like images and videos.

Google Drive, and Amazon S3 are examples of object storage.

Both SQL and noSQL databases are not ideal for large objects. They're best for objects that are a few kilobytes each, such as strings, integers, and timestamps.

Object storage is a type of key-value storage. For example, when I submit a photo to storage (the value) I might be given back a URL for that photo (the key) that I can use to retrieve the photo again later. These keys are unique.

Object storage can be split across many machines for scaling purposes.

## NoSQL

The domain of non-relational databases that use varying query languages to access and handle data within a database.

## SQL

SQL stands for structured query language. It's used to extract information from a relational database. To demonstrate an example SQL query, let's use this table as an example:

| \multicolumn{3}{c}{USERS} |||
| --- | --- | --- |
| user_id | username | enabled |
| 1 | "Harry Potter" | True |
| 2 | "Lord Voldemort" | False |

Let's run the following query on this table:

```
SELECT username, enabled FROM USERS
WHERE username = "Harry Potter"
```

- SELECT indicates which fields to extract from the database.
- FROM indicates which table to query.

- WHERE states the criteria for selecting rows of data.

So, the query above extracts the following information:

| username | enabled |
|---|---|
| Harry Potter | true |

The fourth most common SQL command is the JOIN command. JOIN allows one to query information across two tables matching a value in a common field.

Now, given these tables:

| USERS | | |
|---|---|---|
| user_id | username | enabled |
| 1 | "Harry Potter" | True |
| 2 | "Lord Voldemort" | False |

| MAGIC | |
|---|---|
| user_id | spell |
| 1 | positivemagic |
| 2 | negativemagic |

Let's run the following query on this scenario:

SELECT USERS.username, MAGIC.spell FROM USERS INNER JOIN MAGIC ON MAGIC.user_id=USERS.user_id WHERE USERS.username = "Harry Potter"

The query above extracts the following information:

| username | spell |
|---|---|
| Harry Potter | positivemagic |

We joined both tables on user_id since each user has its own, unique identifier.

# Cloud Architecture

Here are some concepts you should know related to cloud architecture. It maps closely with the sixth step of the PEDALS framework, Scale.

## Application Server

Application servers are simply servers that host applications.

## Cloud Terms

Understanding cloud terminology helps during the architectural component of PEDALS. Here, we cover cloud computing terminology on the three most popular platforms:

- Amazon Web Services (AWS)
- Microsoft Azure
- Google Cloud (GCP)

### Service Summary Across Vendors

|  | Amazon | Microsoft | Google |
|---|---|---|---|
| **Compute** | EC2 | Virtual Machine | Compute Engine |
| **Load Balancing** | Elastic Load Balancing | Azure Load Balancer | Cloud Load Balancing |
| **Serverless Computing** | Lambda Functions | Azure Functions | Cloud Functions |
| **Containers** | Elastic Container Service | Azure Kubernetes | Google Kubernetes |
| **Object Storage** | S3 | Azure Storage (Blob) | Google Cloud Storage |

## Compute

Compute refers to cloud resources, typically server CPUs, to run your code in the cloud.

## Load Balancers

Load balancers redirect user traffic to different compute instances, so an overall system can support more servers.

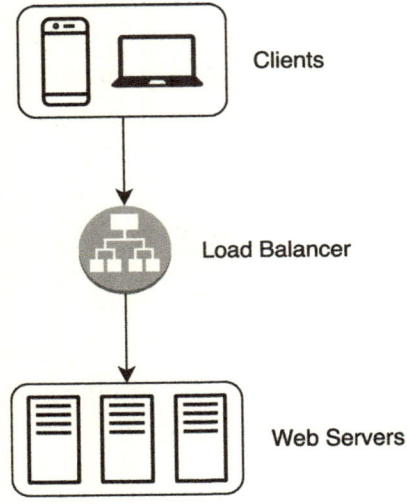

Doing so improves overall system responsiveness and availability.

Because load balancers can redirect traffic, it also prevents a single server from becoming a single point of failure.

## Load Balancing Algorithms

Load balancers can intelligently distribute incoming requests to servers in different ways. We call these load balancing algorithms. Here are the most common load balancing algorithms:

| Strategy | Description |
|---|---|
| Round Robin (RR) | Cycle through the available servers fairly, in a predetermined order, to evenly distribute requests. RR does not consider the magnitude/size of the request and performs an even distribution. |
| Least Connections (LC) | LCM forwards the current request to the server with the fewest number of active connections. Pass the request to the server that is currently servicing the least number of requests. |
| Least Response (LR) | LR sends the request to the server with the least active connections and the least average response time. |
| Least Bandwidth (LB) | LB sends the request to the server with the least amount of traffic. |
| Chained Failover (CF) | CF has an array of servers to choose from. Start at the first server, keep forwarding requests to a single server until it cannot accept any more requests. Then, proceed to the next server in the list and continue to do so and so on. |
| IP Hash | IP Hash determines the assigned server based on a hash of the IP address. This is important if a client needs to connect to a session that is still active after being disconnected and reconnected. |

## Serverless Compute

Event-driven, serverless computing runs stand-alone on a cloud provider's servers without managing servers. In a way, this is a throwback to the mainframe model where many clients would submit code to be run, but not have control over when exactly the mainframe would run their code.

There's no need to worry about hardware or scaling. Providers charge per execution, based on actual computing resources used. When analyzed at a per unit of time scale, serverless computing is usually more expensive than dedicated server resources.

A common use case of serverless computing is when an application's traffic pattern is irregular or unstable. For example, look at an NFL scoring system. Users tend to look up the score of a game most often when the game is taking place. Having a dedicated server running on most non-game days is not worth the money. In turn, serverless computing would be a good opportunity to only compute information when it is requested.

## Containers

Containers allow your code to run within an isolated environment, making your code and compute instances machine agnostic. Through this, containers provide portability and security.

## Object/Block Storage

Object and block storage systems allow clients to store immense files on the cloud without having to worry about maintaining the file or a file system. Cloud providers internally store the file and generate a unique identifier for the object, which is later used to retrieve the object from the cloud provider.

## Orchestration Service

Orchestration services allow for the rapid progression and stable support of web applications. These services automatically manage to compute and storage services for your application, scaling up and down depending on user growth.

For example, AWS offers Elastic BeanStalk, which provides automatic service management for an EC2, S3, ELB, etc. Orchestration services can remove significant overhead and boilerplate work for an engineering team.

## HTTP

HTTP stands for Hypertext Transfer Protocol. HTTP is how data is transferred across the web.

HTTPS is the secure version of HTTP. All HTTPS traffic is encrypted so no third party can read or change the message.

## Internet Protocol (IP)

Internet Protocol states that each IP Packet has an IP Header that contains the recipient's IP Address.

## IP Address

An IP address identifies a website or device on the internet such as 192.168.1.1.

IP stands for Internet Protocol. IP standardizes networking protocols so different machines can connect and transfer information via a transfer protocol, such as TCP or UDP.

The two most discussed IP versions are IPv4 and IPv6. IPv6 was invented primarily due to fears that IP addresses would run out on the IPv4 standard.

The main difference between the two:

- IPv4 has a 32-bit address space, which limits it to 3.7 billion unique IPv4 addresses.
- IPv6 has a 128-bit address space, which limits it to 340 undecillion (or trillion trillion trillion) IPv6 addresses.

## IP Packet

An IP packet is a small segment of information traveling over the internet.

Each packet starts with a header to demarcate the following:

- Header Size
- Packet Size
- Time to Live (TTL)*
- Type of Transport Protocol

*TTL is the number of network hops the IP packet can make before being discarded.

| 0 | | 8 | 16 | | 24 | 32 |
|---|---|---|---|---|---|---|
| Version (4 bits) | IHL (4 bits) | | Type Of Service (TOS) (8 bits) | | Total Length (TL) (4 bits) | |
| Identification (16 bits) | | | | Flags (3 bits) | Fragment Offset (13 bits) | |
| Time To Live (TTL) (8 bits) | | | Protocol (8 bits) | | Header Checksum (16 bits) | |
| Source Address (32 bits) | | | | | | |
| Destination Address (32 bits) | | | | | | |
| Option (0 - 40 bits) | | | | | | |
| Data | | | | | | |

Screenshot / QuestionSolves

## Physical Design

A system's physical design specifies the system hardware and how it's distributed across the system.

A physical design doesn't specify the data flows, but a logical design does.

## Transmission Control Protocol (TCP)

TCP stands for transmission control protocol. TCP provides a specific method and structure of sending packets over an IP network. It structures information and data packets sent over the internet. TCP provides the following:

### Ordered Packets

The receiver knows the exact order, out of the total transmission, that a packet belongs in.

### Confirmation

Receivers send "acknowledgments" to the sender for every packet they receive. This ensures that there are no missing packets.

## Congestion Control

TCP controls the rate at which data is transmitted between the sender and receiver to avoid network collapses due to exterior constraints

## TCP vs. UDP

UDP, or user datagram protocol, is another way to send packets across an IP network.

UDP is often compared with TCP. Each one has advantages and disadvantages; the choice to use one over another depends on the situation:

|  | TCP | UDP |
| --- | --- | --- |
| **Reliable** | Yes<br>Checks for dropped packets. Packets are "acknowledged" by the receiver, so both parties know which information was not transmitted. | No<br>The receiver doesn't know it did not receive packets.<br><br>Packets are not acknowledged, so there are no checks for dropped packets. |
| **Sequential Order** | Yes<br>Data packets in TCP are received in a guaranteed, successive order. | No<br>Datagrams in UDP are not guaranteed to be received in the order sent. |
| **Connection Weight** | Heavy<br>TCP requires many packets to establish a connection to start transmission. However, it provides reliability, ordering, and congestion control. | Light<br>UDP does not establish a connection between two machines. It blindly transfers information across an internet connection. Does not track messages. |
| **Connection Type** | 1-to-1 communication<br>TCP can only communicate between two endpoints. Data cannot be transferred to multiple recipients at the same time. | Broadcast communication<br>UDP allows a singly sent packet to be received by multiple recipients since it does not establish a connection. |

Most websites use TCP transmission. SSH connections also use TCP.

UDP is used by streaming applications such as Skype and Facetime.

## User Datagram Protocol (UDP)

The user datagram protocol, or UDP, provides a set structure of how information can be relayed across internet connections. Here's how it works:

UDP sends "datagrams" across internet connections as its single unit of data. Datagrams are basic transfer units, which have a header and a payload.

UDP is known for the following characteristics:

### Broadcast/Multicast
A single datagram can be sent to multiple machines at the same time without extra work

### Lightweight Data Transfer
UDP does not verify ordering or receipt of data transmission, which allows for faster transfer times across connections

Note: To compare the two most common Internet Protocol examples, take a look at *TCP vs. UDP.*

## Web Servers
Web servers store, process, and deliver web pages to clients. Web servers primarily server HTML documents using the HTTP protocol.

# Scaling
Here are some concepts you should know related to scaling a system. It maps closely with the sixth step of the PEDALS framework, Scale.

## Caching
Caching is about saving requested data to a faster or closer data store so that data can be accessed again in the future.

Caching takes advantage of the locality of reference, which is the tendency to access the same information over and over again.

Caching offers the following benefits:

- Reduces user wait time
- Saves network bandwidth
- Eliminates unnecessary computation time

Caching feels similar to load balancing. However, load balancing typically involves the usage of additional servers which is known as scaling horizontally. Caching usually does not.

## Reading from Cache

When reading from the cache, sometimes the requested data is there. Sometimes not. We refer to this data *availability* as a cache hit or miss:

|  | Definition | System response |
|---|---|---|
| Cache Hit | Data is available in the cache. | Respond to the external data request by using the cached data. |
| Cache Miss | Data is not available in the cache. | Respond to the external data request by fetching from disk storage, using extra compute and network resources. |

Along with data availability, we care about cache *freshness*. Freshness refers to whether the cache's information is up to date. Out of date, or stale, data can be a concern.

For example, stale bank data can frighten both clients and banks. However, an older version of a personal web page can be less catastrophic.

The most common way cache systems determine freshness is with age. Cache systems often delete cache data that exceed an age threshold, which we call time-to-live (TTL).

## Writing from Cache

Writing new data, with a cache system in place, can be complicated. There are three common cache writing policies:

| Policy | Description | Advantage | Disadvantage |
|---|---|---|---|
| Write-Back | Write to the cache only. | Low latency and high throughput. | Potential data loss, especially if there's a system crash and the only copy is written in the cache. |
| Write-Through | Write to cache and permanent storage at the same time. | Data consistency between cache and storage. | Higher latency. Every write operation has to be done twice. |
| No-Write | Write to permanent storage only. | The cache isn't flooded with write requests. | Higher latency. A read for recently written data will create a cache miss. |

The no-write policy is also known as write-around.

## Replacing the Cache

Caches do not have infinite space, so a cache system dictates rules on what should be removed first. Here are some of the most common policies:

| Policy | Description |
|---|---|
| First In First Out (FIFO) | Discard the block accessed first, regardless of how often it's been accessed |
| Last In First Out (LIFO) | Discard the block accessed last, regardless of how often it's been accessed |
| Least Recently Used (LRU) | Discard the block least recently used |
| Most Recently Used (MRU) | Discard the block most recently used |
| Least Frequently Used (LFU) | Discard the block least frequently used. The system counts how often the block is being used. |
| Random Replacement | Discard a random block |

Cache replacement is also known as cache eviction.

## Chaos Engineering

Chaos engineering is the practice of simulating failure into the development process, even in production environments, intending to prevent failure. Preventing system failure increases customer satisfaction and reduces emergency fixes.

That most famous chaos engineering effort is Chaos Monkey. Developed by Netflix, Chaos Monkey is software that can be configured to deliberately fail servers. It can simulate failures and slowdowns of all kinds and sizes. For example, it can simulate failure of a:

- Payment platform
- Data centers
- Cloud regions

Common chaos engineering solutions include:

- Automated scaling and provisioning
- Extensive system monitoring

## Content Delivery Network (CDN)

CDNs are a network of servers that provide faster access to internet content; CDNs are geographically distributed.

For example, rather than load images and other files from a server in Seattle, it makes more sense for a user in India to load those files from a CDN that's closest to them, such as Indonesia as shown in this example.

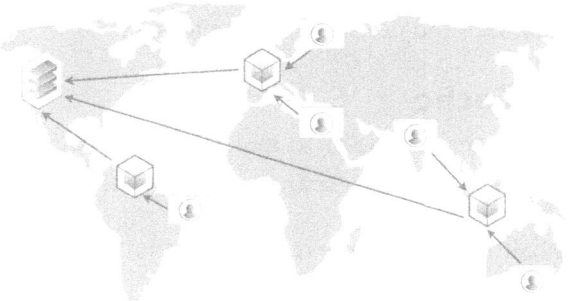

Content Delivery Network (CDN)

Screenshot / Hackernoon

**Advantages of a CDN**
- Lower application server load
- Faster content delivery to users
- Target certain content to certain location-based users

**Disadvantages of a CDN**
- Increased expenditure on software infrastructure
- Adds complexity to software deployment

Geo-location of servers might be misplaced, leading to slower response times from application

## Data Centers

A data center is a dedicated geographic location to house servers and storage systems.

A software application can reside in more than one data center with an eye on serving users from a data center that is closest in proximity to the user. For example, a developer may choose to serve its East Coast users from its Virginia-based data centers rather than its Oregon-based data centers.

When using a multi-data center strategy, a developer must factor how:

- Traffic is routed
- Data is synchronized
- New features and deployments are tested

## Distributed Cache

A traditional cache may reside on a single server. A distributed cache, as its name implies, is a cache that spans multiple servers.

For example, half the cache may reside on server A, and the other half may reside on server B.

Distributed caching is simply an extension of this concept, but the cache is configured to span multiple servers. It's commonly used in cloud computing and virtualized environments, where different servers give a portion of their cache memory into a pool which can then be accessed by virtual machines. A distributed cache is also very scalable.

## Federation

A federated architecture (aka federation) allows two or more systems to interoperate or share information.

## Hadoop Distributed File System (HDFS)

This file system is a distributed network of servers that store files together as a seamless, large file store. HDFS follows conventions that give this distributed file system high reliability and scalability.

## HDFS Terminology

HDFS uses a primary-secondary data architecture. The primary server is called a Namenode. The secondary servers are called Datanodes.

An HDFS usually contains a single Namenode with multiple connected Datanodes.

## How HDFS Works

1. When clients place files in HDFS, they send them through the Namenode.
2. The Namenode orchestrates which Datanodes to write the file to. In HDFS, files are replicated across multiple Datanodes.
3. Namenode stores the metadata about where certain files are located.
4. Retrieval of the file occurs through the Namenode, which knows the exact location of the file (in which Datanode the file is stored in).

HDFS Architecture

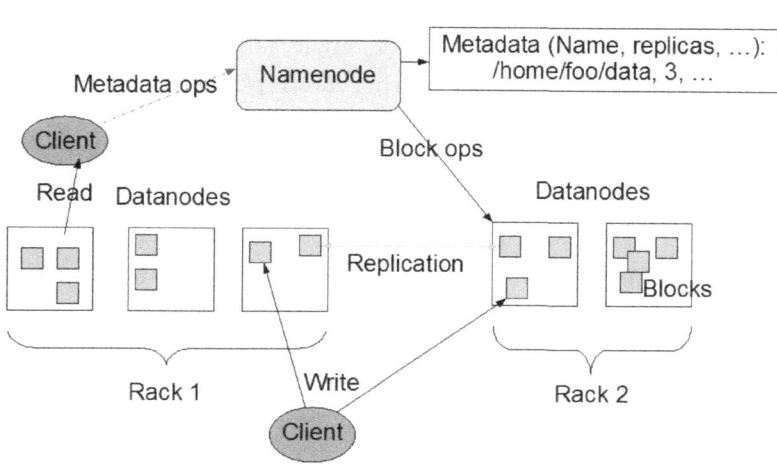

*Diagram of HDFS Architecture*

Screenshot / Madhavi Vaidya

## Horizontal and Vertical Scaling

There are two main ways to scale your physical systems:

- **Vertical Scaling.** Vertical scaling is moving software to a more powerful (single) machine. That machine could have more memory, more storage, or faster CPUs.
- **Horizontal Scaling.** Horizontal scaling is running software across multiple machines.

### Challenges with Vertical Scaling

It's straightforward to upgrade a server's memory, storage, or CPUs. However, there are a few drawbacks to this approach:

- **Cost.** The fastest CPUs, along with the biggest memory and storage upgrades, are very expensive. The ROI decreases as you pursue the best upgrades. In other words, you get diminishing returns.
- **Physical Limitations.** After a certain point, CPUs, memory, and storage cannot be increased further, regardless of cost.
- **Application Size.** Your application may be too intensive to be processed or stored on a single computer, regardless of cost.
- **Single point of failure.** A single large server can suffer a disruption of service during both planned and unplanned downtime.

### Challenges with Horizontal Scaling

Horizontal scaling is almost the de facto approach to scaling applications, given its availability, cost, and redundancy advantages.

However, applications that support horizontal scaling are complex to develop and the information across horizontal databases may not be consistent with one another.

# MapReduce

## What is MapReduce?
MapReduce divides work among multiple computers.

These computers can do the work in parallel; this is the Map phase of MapReduce.

When the work is complete, a final compilation or summary is performed; this is the reduce phase of MapReduce.

Apache Hadoop and Apache CouchDB are popular, open-source MapReduce frameworks.

## Why use MapReduce?
MapReduces speeds up the time it takes to process large amounts of data.

## MapReduce Examples

### Example 1: Search
Consider a search over billions of pages: It would take too long on a single computer. With MapReduce, many computers can search a subset of pages and then return the partial result to the Reducer. The Reducer can then combine it with other partial results before presenting the final results to the user.

### Example 2: Sorting
MapReduce is useful for sorting. Unsorted data can be distributed to a cluster and given to a reducer, which can merge the sorted partial results faster.

### Example 3: System Processes
MapReduce can be used to divide work between processes on a single machine. Querying a database with millions of records is much faster when multiple worker processes search assigned portions of the database in parallel.

**Example 4: Processing Data**
MapReduce also processes and transforms data. A photo-sharing service can automatically generate thumbnails for users' images. When creating an album, the thumbnails can be created in parallel on many machines (Map) and then combined on the web page (Reduce).

## Sharding
Sharding splits a single large database, typically residing on a single server, into smaller databases across multiple servers.

## Zookeeper (Apache)
Apache Zookeeper makes it easier to manage a large set of distribute servers. Here are some benefits that Zookeeper provides:

- **Naming**. Zookeeper allows nodes to be called by a name.
- **Cluster management**. Zookeeper coordinates how nodes can join and leave clusters.
- **Status**. Zookeeper maintains node status.
- **Leader election**. Zookeeper manages the election of a lead node.
- **Configuration management**. Zookeeper maintains configuration information and integrity across the system.

# Chapter 12 Frequently Asked Questions

## Does the interviewer impact the question I get?
Interviewers often choose familiar system design problems. As a result, their questions often relate to their day-to-day work.

Research your interviewer's projects and responsibilities, both past and present, for potential areas of discussion.

Interviewers also tend to ask trendy questions. Those questions can be inspired by a popular product or a recent engineering blog post.

## Does the company impact the question I get?
Companies can influence interviewers' questions. Their questions may originate from:

- Sample questions suggested in *company documentation*
- Questions shared by *peers*
- Questions inspired by the company's *preferred technology stacks*
- Questions inspired by the company's *clients* or *partners*

Your best bet is to find an internal contact who can give insight on popular questions to prepare for. You might even get lucky; they might send you a question list too.

## How do questions vary at Google, Facebook, and Amazon?
These three companies are some of the most coveted employers in the technology sector. And they do have some interview patterns you should be aware of:

**Google & Amazon**
Both companies focus on building Internet applications serving millions and sometimes billions of users. Therefore, expect and prepare for system design questions.

One quirk about Google: they're more likely to ask you to design a Google product such as:

- *Design YouTube.*
- *Design Google Search.*
- *Design Google Maps.*

Amazon, like other companies, is more likely to ask you to design non-Amazon products.

### Facebook
Facebook's interview process has three areas, each with a colorful name:

- **Jedi**. The "Jedi" interview consists of behavioral interview questions to assess your culture fit.
- **Ninja**. The "Ninja" interview consists of coding interview questions.
- **Pirate**. The "Pirate" interview consists of system design interview questions.

Facebook candidates typically get two Ninja interviews and one Jedi interview. Experienced candidates also receive a Pirate interview.

## Do small companies ask system design questions more often?
We do not see a meaningful difference between the likelihood of system design questions between small and large companies.

## Should I ask friends what questions to expect?
Yes. This is the most important tip of all: ask your recruiter, hiring manager, and friends – at the target company – what you should expect. You'll be more efficient in your preparation.

## How much time do I have to complete a system design interview question?
This can vary depending on the interviewer and the company.

In general, we expect the typical system design interview to take between 30 and 60 minutes.

If you have any doubts, ask your interviewer. For example, we would ask him, "In building this system, did you want my brief thoughts over 5 minutes? Or do I have something closer to 45 minutes so I can go into detail?"

## How much time should I spend on each step of the PEDALS method?

Here are our suggestions:

| Step | Time |
| --- | --- |
| Process requirements | 3 to 5 minutes |
| Estimate | 5 minutes |
| Design the service | 10 minutes |
| Articulate the data model | 5 to 10 minutes |
| List the architecture components | 5 minutes |
| Scale | 5 to 10 minutes |

## I try to ask clarifying questions, but the interviewer isn't helpful. What should I do?

Asking clarifying questions is critical to your success in the interview. However, it can sometimes be frustrating when your interviewer's answer is more ambiguous than helpful. The problem often lies in the interviewee asking questions that are too open-ended, such as:

- What services should we consider?
- Which subsystem should I start with?
- How many videos should be uploaded per month?

If the interviewer isn't helpful, it's not because she doesn't want you to succeed. She doesn't want to give you details because she feels like she's doing your work. As mentioned earlier, some interviewees are more willing to help you, while others expect you to take a stronger lead. It's safer to assume the latter.

One more tip: get the interviewer's buy-in for your assumptions. You don't want to use numbers that damage your credibility.

## Some interviewers give many clues. Others don't. What should I expect?

You're right. Every interviewer will have a different approach. Some interviewers provide tips and prompts that makes it easier to get to a solution.

At worst, expect to lead the conversation on your own. All interviewers prefer if you *lead* the technical discussion. Good candidates don't merely participate.

Showcase your communication and leadership skills.

And you don't need the interviewer's prompts. Use PEDALS instead. It's an excellent roadmap for how that conversation should unfold.

## What should I do if the interviewer only gives me 15 minutes?

PEDALS will still work, but you will need to abbreviate your approach.

With only 15 minutes, we'd recommend:

1. Understand the requirements (3 minutes)
2. Design the service (5 minutes)
3. Draw the architecture (5 minutes)

Lastly, to make sure you don't rush unnecessarily, ask the interviewer, during your answer, if she can follow you and if she wants you to go into more detail.

## How can I tell if a question is a system design question? I received a question on "Design an elevator" and "Design an air traffic control system." They sound like system design questions, but after examining them more closely, it seems more like an algorithm question.

Many system design questions could be considered algorithm questions. This might be the case if the system's "service" details are emphasized more than the physical architecture.

Your best bet is to clarify with the interviewer and adjust the PEDALS framework as appropriate. For example, you can skip the "estimation" or "list the architectural components" steps if that's what the interviewer wants.

## The interviewer asked me about an algorithm within a system design question. Is this common?

Algorithm questions can occur within a system design question. For example, the answer to the auto-suggest question uses a trie data structure.

It's worthwhile to review common data structures like arrays, hash tables, trees, and tries. We've also included a Big O time complexity cheat sheet here:

| Notation | Description | Example | Also known as |
|---|---|---|---|
| $O(1)$ | Speed doesn't depend on dataset size | Looking up an item in an array | Constant time |
| $O(\log n)$ | 10x the data = 2x more time | Find item in a sorted array (binary search) | Logarithmic time |
| $O(n)$ | 10x the data = 10x more time | Searching an unsorted array | Linear time |
| $O(n \log n)$ | 10x the data = 20x the time | Nested for loop where inner loop runs in log n time | Log-linear time |
| $O(n^2)$ | 10x the data = 100x more time | Nested for loop, where inner loop runs in n time | Quadratic time |

## The interviewer asked me how I would identify and eliminate bottlenecks in a system. Is that a system design issue?

Yes. That's the underlying theme of the Scale part of the PEDALS framework: there's a constraint that prevents the system from meeting the users' needs. Your job is to suggest how to overcome these limitations (aka bottlenecks) of the system.

## The interview went well, but I haven't heard back yet. What should I do?

This can be quite normal. Some companies take a while to get back to applicants. It takes time to gather feedback from interviewers as they may be out of the office. Or they need to slow down their hiring process because their business needs have changed.

As you can see, there are many reasons why they may not get back to you quickly, and none of them have to do with your suitability as a candidate.

If a week has passed and you haven't heard back from your recruiter, you should absolutely reach out and ask for an update.

## In hindsight, I realized that I screwed something up in the interview. Should I reach out to my recruiter or the interviewer to clear this up?

If it's a substantial mistake, following up with the right answer is a good idea. It demonstrates self-awareness. It also demonstrates a willingness to do what it takes to make things right.

## How much do I need to use the whiteboard during the interview?

We are big fans of using the whiteboard. It makes your answer easier to follow. It slows down your thinking and gives the other person the chance to capture your whiteboard notes with their smartphone.

Finally, there's something magical about the power of the pen. By standing up in front of a whiteboard, you can be perceived as a thought leader, like a professor.

# Chapter 13 Solutions

This section has answers for various sample questions asked throughout the book.

## Answers: Process Requirements Section

Answers to these questions may vary; however, here is a list of examples of possible follow-up questions:

### Design a ride-sharing system. What clarifying questions would you have?
1. Do we only support one vehicle size?
2. In addition to single rides, do we support carpools?
3. What would the customer journey look like when using this ride-sharing system?

### Design a professional social network. What clarifying questions would you have?
1. How is our professional social network different from a standard social network, like Facebook?
2. How can users interact on this platform?
3. Does this platform have a "News Feed"-like feature?

### Create a competitor to AWS, GCP, or Azure. What clarifying questions would you have?
1. Cloud providers have standard feature sets such as Compute and Storage. How does this competitor differentiate?
2. Does this platform support niche solutions such as Machine Learning in addition to Compute and Storage?

## Answers: Estimate Section

### How many transactions does Amazon have per second in the USA?

**Assumptions**
82M Households in USA

- 330M population / 4 persons per household

**40M Prime Accounts**
- 50% of households have Amazon Prime

**20M Non-Prime Amazon Users**
- 25% of households order from Amazon without Prime

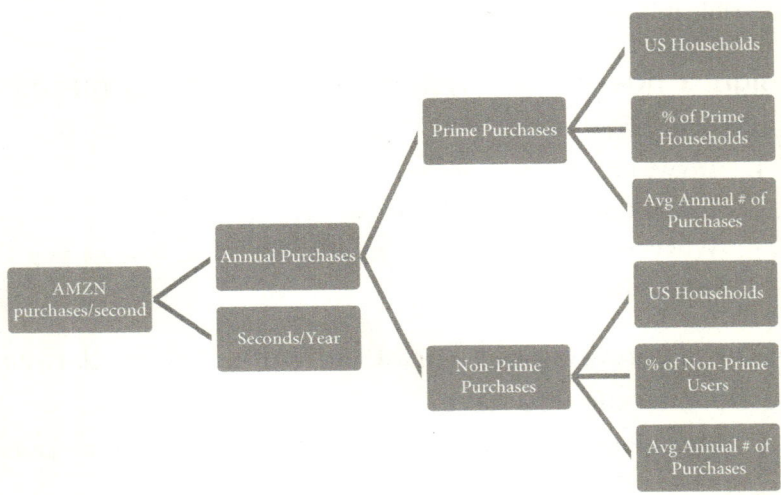

**Calculations**

$$\text{Prime Purch.} = \text{Prime HHs} * \text{Avg Annual Purch.}$$

$$\text{Prime Purchases} = 40M * \frac{52 \text{ purchases}}{\text{year}}$$

**Prime Purchases = 2.08B**

$$\text{NonPrime Purch.} = \text{NonPrime HHs} * \text{Avg Annual Purch.}$$

$$\text{Non Prime Purchases} = 20M * \frac{2.5 \text{ purchases}}{\text{year}}$$

**Non Prime Purchases = 50M**

Annual AMZN Purch. = Prime Purch. + Non Prime Purch.

$$= 2.08B + 50M$$

**Annual AMZN Purchases = 2.13B**

$$\text{AMZN} \frac{\text{Purchases}}{\text{second}} = \text{Annual AMZN Purch.} * \frac{1 \text{ year}}{31536000 \text{ seconds}}$$

$$\text{AMZN} \frac{\text{Purchases}}{\text{second}} = 2.13B * \frac{1 \text{ year}}{31,536,000 \text{ seconds}}$$

$$\text{AMZN} \frac{\text{Purchases}}{\text{second}} \cong 67.54 \frac{\text{purchases}}{\text{second}}$$

**Answer**

There are approximately 67 purchases on Amazon's website per second.

## How many Google searches are executed per second?

**Assumptions**

330M US Population
- 75% of the US has access to Google via smartphones
- 75% of the US has access to Google via computers

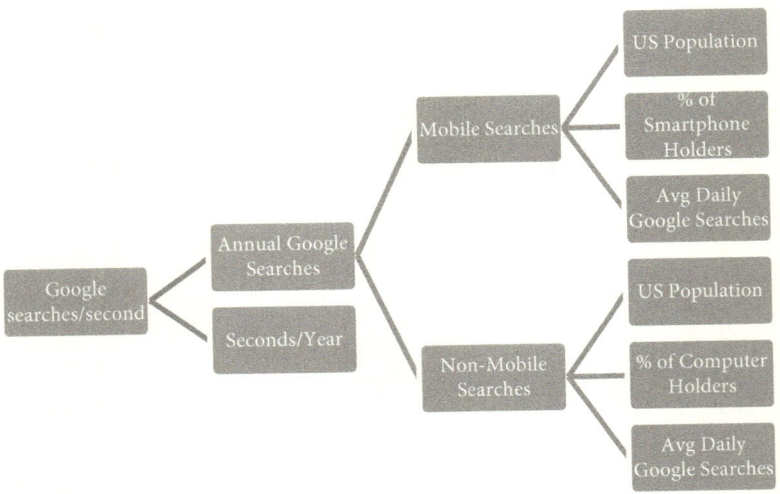

**Calculations**

Daily Mobile Searches
$$= \text{US Pop} * \% \text{ of Smartphone Holders}$$
$$* \text{ Avg Daily Google Searches}$$

$$= 330M * 75\% * 5 \text{ Daily Google Searches (Mobile)}$$

**Daily Mobile Searches = 1.25B**


Non − Mobile Searches
$$= \text{US Pop} * \% \text{ of Computer Holders}$$
$$* \text{ Avg Daily Google Searches}$$

$$= 330M * 75\% * 15 \text{ Daily Google Searches (Non-Mobile)}$$

**Daily Non − Mobile Searches = 3.7B**


Daily Google Searches
$$= \text{Mobile Searches} + \text{Non} - \text{Mobile Searches}$$
$$= 1.25B + 3.7B$$

**Daily Google Searches = ~ 5B**

$$\frac{\text{Google Searches}}{\text{second}} = \text{Daily Google Searches} * \frac{1 \text{ day}}{86{,}400 \text{ seconds}}$$

$$= 5B * \frac{1 \text{ day}}{86{,}400 \text{ seconds}}$$

$$\frac{\text{Google Searches}}{\text{second}} = 57.9K$$

**Answer**
There are approximately 58K searches per second.

# How many WhatsApp messages are transmitted per second in the USA?

**Assumptions**
75% of the US has a smartphone
- ~ 247.5M US smartphone
- ~ 28% of US smartphones are WhatsApp users
- ~ 70M US smartphones have WhatsApp

100 text messages per day per American

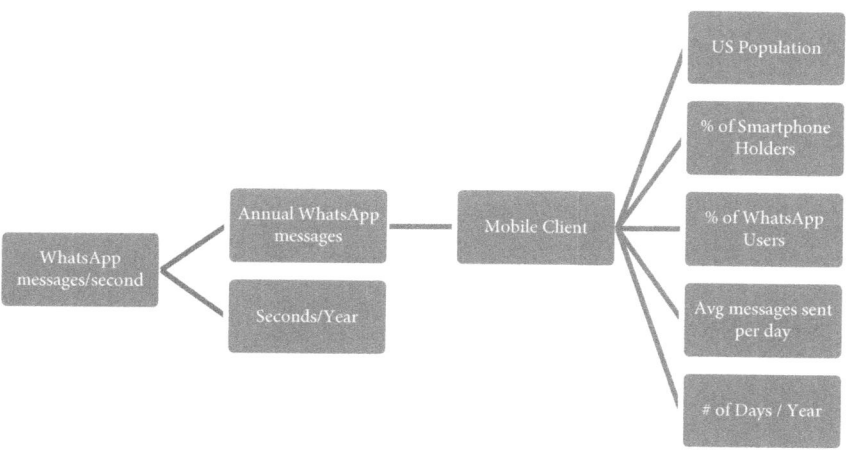

## Calculations

Annual WhatsApp Msgs = US Pop * % ofSmartphone Holders * % of WhatsApp Users * (Messages)/(Day) * # of Days/Year

$$= 330M * 75\% * 28\% 100 * 365$$

**Annual WhatsApp Msgs = 2.5T**

$$\frac{\text{WhatsApp Msgs}}{\text{Second}} = \text{WhatsApp} \frac{\text{Msgs}}{\text{Year}} * \frac{1 \text{ Year}}{31{,}536{,}000 \text{ seconds}}$$

$$= 2.5T * \frac{1 \text{ Year}}{31{,}536{,}000 \text{ seconds}}$$

$$\frac{\text{WhatsApp Msgs}}{\text{Second}} = \sim \frac{80K \text{ messages}}{1 \text{ second}}$$

## Answer

WhatsApp transmits 80K messages per second in the US.

# How much space does Instagram need to store its photos on a given day?

## Assumptions

- We are only counting server-side, not client-side, storage.
- Instagram has roughly 1B users around the world
- ~25% of users upload photos on Instagram
- Average number of photos posted per user annually = 5
- Assume average photo file size is 200 KB

Total # Photos Uploaded Annually

$$= 1B * 25\% * 5 \text{ Photos Uploaded Per User Annually}$$
$$= 1.25B$$

$$\frac{1.25\text{B Photos Uploaded Annually}}{365 \text{ Days}} = \sim 3.5\text{M}$$

$$3.5\text{M} * 200\text{KB} = 700\text{GB}$$

**Answer**

Instagram requires approximately 700 GB of space for its photos on a given day.

## How much storage space does Twitter need on a given day?

**Assumptions**
- We are only counting server-side, not client-side, storage.
- Twitter has roughly 1B users around the world
    - 20% of users are daily active users
    - 25% of daily active users tweet 1 time a day
- Suppose each daily active user reads 100 tweets daily
    - Assume a single tweet, on average, has 100 char
    - Each char is 2 bytes
- 1 in 20 tweets have an image associated with it at 200KB
- 1 in 100 tweets will have a video associated with it at 2MB

$$200\text{M Daily Active Users} * 25\% * 1 = 50\text{M Tweets Per Day}$$

$$200\text{M Daily Users} * 100 \text{ Tweets Consumed} = 20\text{B Views Per Day}$$

$$2 \text{ Bytes} * 100 \text{ Char} = 200 \text{ Bytes Per Tweet}$$

$$200 \text{ Bytes Per Tweet} * 50 \text{ M New Tweets Per Day} = 10\text{GB Tweet Data Per Day}$$

$$\left(50\text{M Tweets Daily} * \frac{1}{20} * 200\text{KB per image}\right)$$
$$+ \left(50\text{M Tweets Daily} * \frac{1}{100} * 2\text{MB Per Video}\right)$$
$$= 0.5\text{TB} + 1\text{TB} = 1.5\text{TB Per Day}$$

**Tweet Data + Image Data + Video Data** $= 20\text{GB} + 1.5\text{TB}$
$= \sim 1.5\text{TB}$

**Answer**
Twitter requires approximately 1.5 TB of storage every day.

# Answers: Design the Service Section

Your answers may vary, but the general structure should be comparable.

## Design an API for a hotel management system

### /reservations

| HTTP Method | Description | Parameters |
|---|---|---|
| POST | Create a new reservation | • Reservation Date<br>• Reservation Type |
| GET | Retrieve a reservation | • Reservation ID |

### /events

| HTTP Method | Description | Parameters |
|---|---|---|
| POST | Create a new hotel event | • Event Date |
| GET | Retrieve a current hotel event | • Event ID |

### /availability

| HTTP Method | Description | Parameters |
|---|---|---|
| GET | Retrieve room availability | • Date<br>• Room Type |

# Design an API for a university course registration system

### /courses

| HTTP Method | Description | Parameters |
|---|---|---|
| GET | Retrieve courses by department | • Course ID<br>• Dept ID |
| UPDATE | Update course information | • Course ID<br>• Course Name<br>• Course Description<br>• Credits<br>• Dept ID |

### /student-registration

| HTTP Method | Description | Parameters |
|---|---|---|
| GET | Retrieve courses | • Course ID<br>• Dept ID |
| POST | Register student to a particular course | • Student ID<br>• Course ID |

# Design an API for a social media platform

### /user

| HTTP Method | Description | Parameters |
|---|---|---|
| POST | Register a new user | • First Name<br>• Last Name<br>• Email Address<br>• Password<br>• Phone Number<br>• Date of Birth<br>• Gender |
| GET | Retrieve a user | • User ID |
| UPDATE | Update user information | • First Name<br>• Last Name<br>• Email Address<br>• Password<br>• Phone Number<br>• Date of Birth<br>• Gender |

### /following

| HTTP Method | Description | Parameters |
|---|---|---|
| POST | Follow a user | • Source User ID<br>• Destination User ID |
| GET | Retrieve following list | • User ID |

| HTTP Method | Description | Parameters |
|---|---|---|
| DELETE | Unfollow a user | • Source User ID<br>• Destination User ID |

## /event

| HTTP Method | Description | Parameters |
|---|---|---|
| POST | Create an event | • User ID<br>• Event Name<br>• Location<br>• Start Date<br>• End Date<br>• Start Time<br>• End Time |
| GET | Retrieve an event | • Event ID |
| UPDATE | Update event information | • User Id<br>• Event Name<br>• Location<br>• Start date<br>• End Date<br>• Start Time<br>• End Time |

## /feed

| HTTP Method | Description | Parameters |
|---|---|---|
| GET | Retrieve a user's feed | • User ID |

# Design an API for a coffee shop's mobile order software

## /user

| HTTP Method | Description | Parameters |
|---|---|---|
| POST | Register a new user | • First Name<br>• Last Name<br>• Email Address<br>• Password<br>• Smartphone Number<br>• Payment Method<br>• Card Number |
| GET | Retrieve a user | • User ID |
| UPDATE | Update user information | • First Name<br>• Last Name<br>• Email Address<br>• Password<br>• Smartphone Number<br>• Payment Method<br>• Card Number |

## /order

| HTTP Method | Description | Parameters |
|---|---|---|
| POST | Submit a new order | • User ID<br>• Payment Method<br>• Card Number<br>• Date of Payment<br>• Amount of Payment<br>• Goods Purchased |
| GET | Retrieve an order | • Order ID |

# Design an API for a third-party payment platform

## /account

| HTTP Method | Description | Parameters |
|---|---|---|
| POST | Register a new account | • First Name<br>• Last Name<br>• Email Address<br>• Password<br>• Smartphone Number<br>• Payment Method<br>• Card Number |
| GET | Retrieve account information | • Account ID |
| UPDATE | Update account | • First Name<br>• Last Name<br>• Email Address<br>• Password<br>• Smartphone Number<br>• Payment Method<br>• Card Number |

## /account/transaction

| HTTP Method | Description | Parameters |
|---|---|---|
| GET | Retrieve transaction information | • Account ID<br>• Transaction ID |

## /account/balance

| HTTP Method | Description | Parameters |
|---|---|---|
| GET | Retrieve account balance | • Account ID |

## /payment

| HTTP Method | Description | Parameters |
|---|---|---|
| POST | Submit a new payment | • Account ID<br>• Transaction Amount |
| GET | Retrieve a payment | • Account ID |

• Transaction ID

# Design an API for a sports news website

## /user

| HTTP Method | Description | Parameters |
|---|---|---|
| POST | Register a new user | • First Name<br>• Last Name<br>• Email Address<br>• Password |
| GET | Retrieve a user | • User ID |
| UPDATE | Update a user | • User ID<br>• First Name<br>• Last Name<br>• Email Address<br>• Password |

## /user/interests

| HTTP Method | Description | Parameters |
|---|---|---|
| POST | Add a new team interest for the user | • User ID<br>• Team ID<br>• Sport ID |
| GET | Retrieve a user's team interests | • User ID |

## /team

| HTTP Method | Description | Parameters |
|---|---|---|
| POST | Add team information | • Sport ID<br>• Team Info |
| GET | Retrieve team information | • Team ID |
| UPDATE | Update team information | • Team ID<br>• Sport ID<br>• Team Info |

## /search

| HTTP Method | Description | Parameters |
|---|---|---|
| GET | Retrieve search results | • Query Term |

# Answers: Articulate the Data Model Section

What tables and fields would you have for a social media site?

| USERS | |
|---|---|
| User ID (PK) | INT |
| Username (FK) | VARCHAR |
| First Name | VARCHAR |
| Last Name | VARCHAR |
| Gender | ENUM |
| Date of Birth | DATETIME |
| Create Date | DATETIME |
| Cancellation Date | DATETIME |
| Other Details | VARCHAR |

| MESSAGES | |
|---|---|
| Message ID (PK) | INT |
| Username (FK) | VARCHAR |
| Message Text | VARCHAR |
| Message Type Code (FK) | ENUM |
| Date Sent | DATETIME |

| MESSAGE TYPES | |
|---|---|
| Message Type Code (PK) | INT |
| Message Type Description (Likes, Retweet, etc.) | ENUM |

| FOLLOWING | |
|---|---|
| User ID (PK) | INT |
| Usernames | ARRAY |

| FOLLOWERS | |
|---|---|
| Username (PK) | INT |
| Usernames | ARRAY |

What tables and fields would you have for an e-commerce website?

| CUSTOMERS | |
|---|---|
| Customer ID (PK) | INTEGER |
| Customer Name | VARCHAR |
| Customer Phone | INTEGER |

243

| Customer E-Mail | VARCHAR |
|---|---|
| Payment Method | VARCHAR |

| CUSTOMER ADDRESSES | |
|---|---|
| Address ID (PK) | INTEGER |
| Customer ID (FK) | INTEGER |
| Street Address | VARCHAR |
| City | VARCHAR |
| State | VARCHAR |
| Zip | INTEGER |
| Country | VARCHAR |

| CUSTOMER ORDERS | |
|---|---|
| Order ID (PK) | INTEGER |
| Customer ID (FK) | INTEGER |
| Order Date | DATETIME |
| Order Status Code | VARCHAR |

| PRODUCTS | |
|---|---|
| Product ID (PK) | INTEGER |
| Product Name | VARCHAR |
| Product Price | FLOAT |
| Supplier ID (FK) | INTEGER |
| Inventory Count | INTEGER |
| Product Type Code (FK) | VARCHAR |

| PRODUCT TYPES | |
|---|---|
| Product Type Code (PK) | INTEGER |
| Product Type Description | VARCHAR |

| ORDERS | |
|---|---|
| Order ID (PK) | INTEGER |
| Customer ID (FK) | INTEGER |
| Order Date | DATETIME |
| Fulfillment Date | DATETIME |
| Order Status | VARCHAR |

| ORDER ITEMS | |
|---|---|
| Order Item ID (PK) | INTEGER |
| Order ID (FK) | INTEGER |
| Product ID (FK) | INTEGER |
| Item Quantity | INTEGER |

| SUPPLIERS | |
|---|---|
| Supplier ID (PK) | INTEGER |
| Supplier Phone | INTEGER |
| Supplier E-Mail | VARCHAR |

What tables and fields would you have for an airline operations application?

| PASSENGERS | |
|---|---|
| Passenger ID (PK) | INTEGER |
| First Name | VARCHAR |
| Last Name | VARCHAR |
| Phone Number | INTEGER |
| E-Mail | VARCHAR |
| Payment ID (FK) | INTEGER |

| ADDRESS INFORMATION | |
|---|---|
| Address ID (PK) | INTEGER |
| Street Address | VARCHAR |
| City | VARCHAR |
| State | VARCHAR |
| Zip | INTEGER |
| Country | VARCHAR |
| Passenger ID (FK) | INTEGER |

| AIRPORTS | |
|---|---|
| Airport ID (PK) | INTEGER |
| Name | VARCHAR |
| Code | VARCHAR |
| City | VARCHAR |
| State | VARCHAR |

| FLIGHT SCHEDULES | |
|---|---|
| Flight Path ID (PK) | INTEGER |
| Origin Airport ID (FK) | INTEGER |
| Destination Airport ID (FK) | INTEGER |
| Departure Time | DATETIME |
| Arrival Time | DATETIME |

| RESERVATIONS | |
|---|---|
| Reservation ID (PK) | INTEGER |
| Passenger ID (FK) | INTEGER |
| Flight Path ID (FK) | INTEGER |

| Passenger Count | INTEGER |
|---|---|

| PAYMENT | |
|---|---|
| Payment ID (PK) | INTEGER |
| Passenger ID (FK) | INTEGER |
| Credit Card Type | VARCHAR |
| Credit Card Information (Encoded) | VARCHAR |

## What tables and fields would you have for a ride-sharing application?

| RIDERS | |
|---|---|
| Rider ID (PK) | INTEGER |
| First Name | VARCHAR |
| Last Name | VARCHAR |
| Point Balance | INTEGER |
| Payment ID (FK) | INTEGER |

| DRIVERS | |
|---|---|
| Driver ID (PK) | INTEGER |
| First Name | VARCHAR |
| Last Name | VARCHAR |
| Phone Number | INTEGER |
| Vehicle Type | VARCHAR |
| Employment ID (FK) | INTEGER |

| EMPLOYMENT INFO | |
|---|---|
| Employment Info ID (PK) | INTEGER |
| Driver ID (FK) | INTEGER |
| SSN (Encoded) | VARCHAR |
| Address | VARCHAR |
| City | VARCHAR |
| State | VARCHAR |
| Zip | VARCHAR |

| PAYMENTS | |
|---|---|
| Payment ID (PK) | INTEGER |
| Rider ID (FK) | INTEGER |
| Credit Card Type | VARCHAR |
| Credit Card Information (Encoded) | VARCHAR |

| RIDE HISTORY | |
|---|---|

| | |
|---|---|
| Ride ID (PK) | INTEGER |
| Rider ID (FK) | INTEGER |
| Driver ID (FK) | INTEGER |
| Ride Call Time | DATETIME |
| Pick-Up Location | VARCHAR |
| Drop-Off Location | VARCHAR |
| Trip Duration | FLOAT |
| Trip Distance | FLOAT |
| Trip Cost | FLOAT |

# Answers: Scale Section

Your answers may vary, but the general structure should be comparable.

## How would you address these scalability situations?

**Rapid user base growth**
- Horizontal Scaling
- CDN for media content
- Database sharding as database capacity nears limits

**Peak demand like Black Friday and New Years**
- Auto-scaling
- Selecting a new load balancing heuristic

**Users complaining about slow response times**
- Caching DB responses
- CDN for media content
- Increased horizontal scaling

## Which sharding strategies minimize future work?

A range-based strategy is simple and does not require large overhaul of the database and sharding system.

A modular-based sharding system is subject to large-scale overhaul by reproportioning data distribution.

# What's Next

Thanks for reading! However, our journey doesn't end here. First, we'd love to hear from you. Please send questions, comments, typos and edits to: lewis@impactinterview.com.

Second, we have three more resources for you:

- Visit Lewis' website, lewis-lin.com. You'll find more resources to help you prepare.
- Sign-up for Lewis' newsletter. I send articles, interview tips and new sample answers that you'll find helpful in your interviews. Sign-up at lewis-lin.com.
- Find a practice partner. You can find practice partners at my Slack group. To sign up, search for "Lewis Lin Slack" on Google. If system design doesn't come naturally to you, the most effective way to nail them is practice!

Finally, **we have a favor to ask you. Please take a moment to review the book on Amazon**. Whether you loved or hated the book, you can help us improve subsequent editions by writing an Amazon review.

Book reviews also play an important in promoting the book to a larger audience, which in turn give us a bigger opportunity to create better interview preparation materials for you in the future.

Thank you for reading and reviewing *The System Design Interview*. May you get the job of your dreams!

*Lewis C. Lin & Shivam P. Patel*

# Acknowledgments

A big thank you goes to everyone involved in the book. We couldn't have done this without your feedback, thoughts, and brainstorming. If we left out any of you, we apologize for the inadvertent exclusion.

Abbie Austin

Adam Loving

Ardeley Sihite

Chris Schattauer

David Lim

Erin Sovereign

Ian M. Bone

Kendall Miller

Kevin Lin

Kristen Cho

Paul Boudreaux

Robert Wlodarczyk

Valerie Chan

Made in the USA
Middletown, DE
23 September 2024

61322348R00149